MW00528788

THE APPRAISAL OF APARTMENT BUILDINGS

THE APPRAISAL OF APARTMENT BUILDINGS

DANIEL J. O'CONNELL, MAI

John Wiley & Sons, Inc.

New York • Chichester • Brisbane • Toronto • Singapore

Library of Congress Cataloging in Publication Data:

O'Connell, Daniel J.

The appraisal of apartment buildings / by Daniel J. O'Connell.

p. cm.

Bibliography: p.

ISBN 0-471-50955-8

1. Apartment houses—Valuation. 2. Real property—Valuation. I. Title.

HD1387.037 1989 89-5511

336.22'5—dc19 CIP

Printed in the United States of America

10 9 8 7 6 5 4 3 2 1

FOREWORD

The proper completion of an apartment appraisal report is a difficult assignment at best considering the many factors that must be taken into account. Apartment appraisals must comply not only with all of the basic requirements of the appraisal process but must also incorporate, when required, such factors as the recognition of rent control and rental concessions, the inclusion of a cash flow analysis and compliance with Federal Regulatory Appraisal Regulations as examples. In addition, both current and future competition for the subject property must be accounted for because these factors can have a significant impact on the absorption, vacancy and success or failure of a project.

The Appraisal of Apartment Buildings, by Daniel J. O'Connell, MAI, provides a comprehensive guide to help staff and fee appraisers, lenders, investors, and real estate brokers understand what should be included in a well researched, thoroughly analyzed and properly documented appraisal report on apartment properties. Mr. O'Connell's book draws upon his extensive apartment appraisal experience with both institutional lenders and as the president of a fee appraisal firm that specializes exclusively in the appraisal of apartment buildings. His practical experience in the field has enabled him to compile this thorough resource. Taking a practical approach to the subject, the book covers such topics as: inspecting the property, restructuring the rent roll, collecting rental comparables, and reconciling the approaches to value among other subjects. The book includes both good and bad examples of sections of apartment appraisal reports to illustrate the text.

Our Bank thought so highly of *The Appraisal of Apartment Buildings,* that we received authorization and are adapting eight of the chapters to our operation for use in our appraisal manual. We consider Mr. O'Connell's material to be an excellent reference guide on the subject and believe that it is an invaluable aid for anyone involved in the appraisal of apartments.

THOMAS E. O'NEIL, MAI
Vice President
Appraisal Administration
Great Western Bank
Northridge, California

PREFACE

In 1982, John Wiley & Sons published my book entitled *Apartment Building Valuation, Finance and Investment Analysis*. At the time, I was involved in real estate finance and investment for New York Life Insurance Company, and the book, written primarily for investors, was heavily tax oriented. In March 1985 I founded Apartment Building Appraisers and Analysts, Inc., and returned full-time to apartment appraising. Chapter 13, Cash Equivalence, is largely abstracted from that earlier book, as are the Calculator Procedures (Appendix B). All other portions here are new.

The intent of this book is to provide a practical guide for appraisers, lenders, brokers, investors, and others faced with the problem of estimating the value of an apartment building. Also, it should help investors and brokers to better interface with lenders and appraisers.

I've not attempted to cover all the basics of appraising—this is done quite well in *The Appraisal of Real Estate*[1], considered by many to be the appraisal profession's bible. Rather, this book covers the nuances of appraising apartment buildings and the completion of standardized Federal National Mortgage Association (FNMA) apartment appraisal forms. Also, I've taken the opportunity to emphasize the influence that tenancy, management, and finance have on value—topics that have been largely neglected in previous writings.

While the market approach and the income approach to value are covered in this book, the cost approach is omitted due to its inapplicability for many assignments. Highest and best use is the other basic topic not covered; most existing apartment properties are already developed to their highest and best use and, after determining

[1] *The Appraisal of Real Estate,* American Institute of Real Estate Appraisers, Chicago, 1987.

this, no further analysis is required. For those properties that aren't at their highest and best use, the consequent analysis could be well beyond the space limitations of this book.

An appraisal case study of a 50-unit apartment building is used in many of this book's examples and exhibits. This is not meant to be reflective of the finest possible work product—few assignments afford the luxury of unlimited time involvement. It is meant to reflect the type of work which can be performed in a reasonable time and which is acceptable to most clients.

There are an almost infinite number of unique problems which can surface during the appraisal of any piece of real property. These problems include clouds on title; unusual income streams; persistent maintenance or structural problems; asbestos or other hazardous materials on the property; and impending changes in local economic, social, governmental, or environmental forces. If you're unsure of how to deal with such problems, enlist the help of an expert, either a fellow appraiser or another type of professional.

Having been born and raised in Montana's Rocky Mountains, I am very aware of the shortage of guidance and information available to those of you living in sparsely populated areas. I've tried to consider your plight as much as possible, but that doesn't get you out of having the worst situation in which to appraise apartments. You should take special note of the income approach (Chapter 11).

This book was assembled from my own experiences and is, in essence, the book I'd want to issue to appraisers joining my company. I hope that it will help you produce good reports and gain the respect of those who read them.

DANIEL J. O'CONNELL, MAI

Woodland Hills, California
July 1989

CONTENTS

THE APPRAISAL OF APARTMENT BUILDINGS

PART ONE

CHAPTER ONE

AN OVERVIEW

DEFINITION OF MARKET VALUE

As used in this book, *value* refers to *market value*. Other types of value include investment value, assessed value, and insurable value. While various sources (courts, regulatory organizations, texts, etc.) offer various definitions of market value, almost all of thèm describe an arm's-length transaction with a willing buyer and willing seller, no undue pressure on either party, and no special financing considerations.

The most popular definition of market value is the one approved by the Federal Home Loan Bank as of this writing:

> The most probable price which a property should bring in a competitive and open market under all conditions requisite to a fair sale, with the buyer and seller each acting prudently and knowledgeably, and assuming the price is not affected by undue stimulus. Implicit in this definition is the consummation of a sale as of a specified date and the passing of title from the seller to buyer under conditions whereby:
>
> **1.** Buyer and seller are typically motivated;
> **2.** Both parties are well informed or well advised, and each is acting in what he or she considers his or her own best interest;
> **3.** A reasonable time is allowed for exposure in the open market
> **4.** Payment is made in terms of cash in U.S. dollars or in terms of financial arrangements comparable thereto; and
> **5.** The price represents a normal consideration for the property sold, unaffected by special or creative financing or sales concessions granted by anyone associated with the sale.

MANAGEMENT

Everything else being equal (including income), investors will most often pay substantially more for the same property if it is well managed and a has a good tenancy. Yet management and tenancy are rarely discussed in appraisal reports. For instance, Form 71A, the most in-depth of the standard appraisal forms, does not explicitly call for any discussion of the quality of management or tenancy. Various chapters in this book note the importance of these items and emphasize their discussion in written reports. A blank sample of a Form 71A is included in this book as Appendix C.

FINANCING

Financing is another topic that receives little emphasis in appraisal literature. However, financing typically constitutes from 75 to 90 percent of the purchase price, and the amount of the loan and its payments are extremely important to the investor when determining how much to pay for the property. Almost all apartment building purchases are heavily dependent on the financing available.

While assumptions regarding specific financing proposals are not directly incorporated into the traditional appraisal techniques, their importance is such that an entire chapter (14) consists of a discussion of loan types and underwriting. Further, the reduction of financing terms to their cash-equivalent value is discussed in Chapter 13.

THE THREE APPROACHES TO VALUE ESTIMATION

There are three classical approaches in real estate appraisal—cost approach, market approach, and income approach, which together are reconciled into the final estimate of fair market value.

Cost Approach

This technique sums the value of the land and the value of the depreciated improvements to arrive at an estimate of market value. It is the least used of the three approaches, due to the following weaknesses:

1. Applying the cost approach to existing properties requires an estimation of the improvements' accrued depreciation due to physical deterioration, func-

tional obsolescence, and locational factors. For older properties, at least, depreciation is quite difficult to estimate accurately.

2. The reproduction or replacement cost of the improvements must be estimated—another process that is subject to inaccuracies.
3. Apartment building investors, especially those buying smaller buildings, are most often interested in buying only existing properties and do not seriously consider the alternative of building a substitute property. This principle of substitution is basic to the validity of the cost approach and its application.
4. Appraisers have become more vocal in questioning the economic theories behind the cost approach and whether separate estimates of land value and building cost really do equate to market value.
5. City zoning regulations, which control the number of units which can be developed on a site, often change over the years. Appraising a parcel upon which a 20-unit apartment sits, but which today could not be redeveloped with more than 10 units, makes the estimation of land value very difficult and suspect.

Had enough? Partially for these reasons, and because the cost approach is well covered in *The Appraisal of Real Estate*, it is omitted from further discussion in this book. Also, relatively little methodology in the cost approach is unique to apartment buildings.

Market Approach

Also known as the sales comparison approach, this method compares the subject property to similar properties which have recently sold in the same geographic area. After researching the characteristics of each comparable property and the particulars of its sale transaction, value indicators based on sales price are abstracted and then applied to the subject. As such, the market approach follows the comparative shopping logic that investors often use when determining the price they will pay for a property.

Income Approach

The income approach uses a capitalization process to convert a property's income stream into a value estimate. While there are various types of capitalization processes, the one most often used for all types of income-producing real estate is the direct capitalization process, in which a rate of return (known as the "overall rate") is applied to a single year's estimate of income.

Affordable hand-held financial calculators became available in the mid-1970s and popularized the discounted cashflow method for estimating value. Again, a rate of return is used but it is applied to a projected series of annual cashflows rather than a single year's income. As it is impossible to abstract a currently applicable rate from sale comparables, discounted cashflow has not achieved the credibility of the other techniques. Still, it is sometimes used by investors (mostly for the acquisition of larger properties) and is occasionally required by lending institutions as a part of the appraisal. As such, it has become an important part of income property appraisal and is discussed in Chapter 16.

DIFFERENT TYPES OF BUYERS

An investor's perception of economic incentive must be understood when we appraise apartments. Despite the 1986 Tax Reform Act's dilution of tax benefits, apartments have continued to be a desirable investment in most parts of the country. Reasons for their popularity include:

1. The investor's equity investment can grow at a magnified rate when any portion of the investment is made with borrowed money.
2. Many investors have lived in apartments and feel they are at least somewhat familiar with their management requirements.
3. Well-occupied apartments are considered low-risk investments in many markets.
4. Apartments have a history of generally providing high returns, especially upon resale.
5. Downpayment requirements are often relatively small.
6. Some tax benefits remain.
7. Fixer-uppers and properties that have been poorly managed can have excellent profit potential.

It is important to be familiar with the type of investor to whom the property in question will most likely be sold. Buildings of fewer than 10 units most frequently appeal to mom-and-pop investors. Mid-size buildings are typically the domain of successful professionals or small- to medium-sized partnerships. Currently, larger properties are typically bought by income-oriented public limited partnerships, Japanese entities, and financial institutions.

Each of these groups has different risk and management profiles. Smaller investors typically want a low downpayment and will be actively involved in property management. These purchases create the bulk of sale transactions and are sometimes based on very little sophistication. Investors in mid-size buildings are looking more for investments which make more economic sense (i.e., adequate cashflow), and they are more apt to come up with a larger downpayment. For the larger properties, the number of buyers thins out considerably and investors can often be more selective. The purchaser's acquisition analysis is probably more lengthy and sophisticated. The appraiser should bear in mind the type of investor most likely to buy the property; this often requires the changing of mentality and approach from one assignment to the next.

CHAPTER TWO

PROPERTY INSPECTION

A thorough inspection of the site and improvements is necessary. The inspection is also the time to determine the style and competence of management as well as the quality of tenancy. The property that has been mismanaged and is ripe for a turnaround will appeal to a different group of investors than does the property whose current management program should be continued. When finished with the property inspection, the appraiser should know the number of vacancies, the types of units in most demand, the percentage of the tenants who are married couples, the number of children, types and locations of tenants' employment, the average frequency of turnovers, and so on. We're looking for trends and generalities—exact figures are not necessary. The appraiser should not only obtain this information and consider it in the value estimate, but should also include it in the appraisal report with sufficient clarity and detail.

ARRANGING THE INSPECTION

This should be the easy part. However, aside from setting the appointment there are several other items that must be arranged. Make sure to arrange for the inspection of a sufficient number of units. Most appraisers will ask to see at least one of each of the different kinds of units, but just because two units have the same number of bedrooms does not mean that they are identical. Also, you may wish to see some upper-floor units to check for roof leaks.

Make sure that the client is able to provide the rent roll and operating expense summary by the time the inspection is made. A lack of documentation can hold up the appraisal and decimate work efficiency. If available, a set of building plans, a title report, and a survey should also be obtained.

APPRAISAL PHOTOGRAPHY

Tools for the inspection should include

1. A notebook
2. Measuring tools (25-foot steel tape and a measuring wheel)
3. Graph paper
4. Appraisal form and/or inspection checklist
5. Flashlight
6. Camera

My appraisers use fully automatic 35mm cameras with built-in flash units. These are easy to use and allow for pictures of various items including kitchen and bath fixtures, thereby providing a good indication of building quality, condition, and appeal. Anything that you recommend be repaired should also be photographed. We'll generally provide from 15 to 30 photos of existing properties and their environs. For large properties, a camera with a wide-angle lens is desirable.

You should approach the photographic documentation of the property as though you were sitting in an office on the opposite side of the country and had no familiarity with the property or location. This means taking photographs of the street in both directions. In the photographs, try to show a corner of the subject to provide a reference point. Then photograph the property across the street. If not well depicted in the street photographs, the adjacent properties on both sides of the subject should also be shown. You may wish to include photographs of nearby properties that represent the typical quality, condition, and type of improvements in the area. Finally, any properties in the area which are noted as having a positive or negative effect on the subject should be photographed.

In the appraisal report, photos should be fully captioned—we'll typically provide about a 20-word description. Also, each photo should be numbered so that it can be referenced within the body of the report.

SITE INSPECTION

The top of page 3 on the 71A form calls for certain information about the site. Figure 2.1 provides a completed example. Observations you should remember to make while at the site include:

1. Is the site serviced by all utilities (electricity, gas, telephone, water, and sewer)? Is there a fire hydrant on the site or within a reasonable distance?
2. Is the site situated so that it affords a view?

SITE

Dimensions 150' x 150' Area 22,500 Sq. Ft. or XXXX

Zoning (classification, uses, and densities permitted) R3. Allows one unit per 600 SF of site. Permits single- and multi-family residential. No commercial. Requires two parking spaces per unit.

Present improvements ☐ do ☒ do not conform to zoning regulations.

Highest and best use: ☒ Present use ☐ Other (specify) If vacant highest and best use is as apartments. If over 50% destroyed, site would be limited to 37 units.

Site Improvements: ☒ Public Water ☐ Private Well ☒ Public Sewer ☐ Septic Tank ☒ Storm Sewer ☒ Sidewalk

☒ Curbs ☒ Gutters ☐ Alley ☒ Street Lights ☒ Electricity ☒ Gas

☐ Underground Electricity and Telephone ☐

Access By: ☒ Public Street ☐ Private Road Street Surface: Asphalt

Maintained By: ☒ Municipality ☐ Private Association (attach summary of Association documents)

Ingress and egress (adequacy and safety) Two points, off Wilson and Third. Adequate and safe.

Topography, view amenity, lot drainage, flood condition, slopes, etc. Level topography. No views from grade-level. Drainage is adequate. No soil problems noted.

Easements or encroachments on site and off site (if any) No enroachments or unusual easements are noted.

Is the property located within a HUD Identified Special Flood Hazard Area? No

Favorable or unfavorable conditions not mentioned above including any nonconforming use(s) of present improvements. Subject is a nonconforming legal use due to density of one unit per 450 square feet of site and 1.50/unit on-site parking. Minor on-site parking shortage due to many two-car households at subject and slightly congested street parking. Currently no adverse effect on subjects marketability.

Lot sketch showing lot dimensions, distance to nearest corner, and the location of any nearby detrimental conditions.

(N)

See Assessor's Parcel Map in Adderda.
No nearby detrimental conditions.

DESCRIPTION OF IMPROVEMENTS

ITEM	DESCRIPTION
Foundation	Concrete slab
Basic Structural System	Type V wood frame
Exterior Walls	Stucco w/ wood trim
Roof Covering	Mineral cap sheet
Interior Walls	3/8" drywall
Floor Covering	Carpet, vinyl
Ceiling Heights of Units	Finished Floor to Finished Ceiling is 8 Ft.
Bath Floor and Walls	Vinyl, drywall
Insulation	Fiberglass batt
Soundproofing	No extra measures Adequate
Heating System, Central or Individual & Fuel	Gas wall furnaces with thermostats.
Air Conditioning System, Central or Individual & Fuel	None. Ocean within one mile.
Hot Water Heater(s)	Central, four 100 gal. gas
Built-in Kitchen Appliances	Range and oven, disposal, DW, hood and fan
Elevator (No. 2)	Otis hydraulic, 2,000 l.b.
Plumbing Fixtures	Average quality & condition.
Security Features	Locking pedestrian and vehicular entries. Intercom at front gate wired into phone system with remote gate release.

Construction: ☒ Existing ☐ Proposed ☐ Under Construction Approx. Year Built 1970

Type Project: ☐ Walk-Up ☒ Elevator ☐ Row or Townhouse ☐ Other (Specify) Centercourt

No. of Bldgs. 1 No. of Stories 4 No. of Units 50

Gross Bldg. Area 39,585 Sq. Ft. Density 97 Units per Acre

OVERALL IMPROVEMENT RATING

	Good	Aver.	Fair	Poor
Architectural Attractiveness	X			
Quality of Construction	X			
Condition of Exterior		X+		
Condition of Interior		X		
Rooms Size and Unit Layout		X		
Kitchen Facilities	X			
Closets and Storage		X+		
Soundproofing Adequacy		X		
Insulation Adequacy		X+		
Electrical Service Adequacy		X		

Comment on items rated fair or poor and items not covered above Subject's style, size, age, quality and condition are typical of buildings in this area. Improvements are built to within 10' of lot line. Block wall and wrought iron gates around perimeter. Each unit has a small balcony.

Effective Age 15 Years. Est. Remaining Economic Life 40 Yrs.

PARKING: Total Spaces 75 In Buildings 75 In Garage (separate) 0 In Carport 0 Open (on-site) 0

Parking Ratio 1.50 Space(s)/Unit. Discuss parking adequacy and convenience to apartment units Two-level subterranean garage is elevator serviced. On-site parking is adequate.

Driveways, curbing, sidewalks, lighting (adequacy and condition) All adequate and in average condition. Landscape along perimeter and in center court is mature, well designed and attractive. Automatic sprinklers.

Describe recreational facilities 10' x 25' pool in spacious, well landscaped cetercourt. 15' x 22' unfurnished rec room at 1st floor near pool is currently used by management for storage.

Describe basement, lobby, garage, laundry, and other building items not described above Two laundry rooms, each with eight washers and eight dryers. Main entry is a tunnel at first floor.

Comment if any of the above items or other building items are inadequate or are in below average condition None of the above are inadequate or in below average condition.

Recommended observable repairs: (List repairs, painting, termite treatment, etc. you recommend be made to the improvements to make the property readily marketable; if none, so state). Roof needs replacement (see comments on Page 1 and Photos Nos. 21 and 22). Appraiser's cost estimate is $8,000 to $10,000. No apparent water damage. Manager reports no persistent maintenance problems. Property appraised as-is.

General comments if applicable: Property is individually metered for gas and electricity. Hallways are wide and have good lighting; carpet and paint is in average condition. Except for roof, property reflects good maintenance practice. Two-bedroom units are double-masters and are well suited to roommate situations.

FHLMC Form 71A Rev. 8/77 Page 3 of 8 FNMA Form 1050 Dec. 83

Figure 2.1. Page 3 of the 71A Form

3. Does the contour of the site and/or surrounding area create any drainage or flood problems?
4. Is vehicular access to any on-site parking areas safe and adequate?
5. Are there any easements or encroachments? If so, what are their effects on the site and its improvements?
6. Is the street leading to the site of adequate capacity? What is the surface material (asphalt, concrete, dirt)? What condition is it in?
7. Is there an alley? If so, is it paved?
8. Are curbs and sidewalks installed? Are they asphalt or concrete?
9. Is there any street lighting? Are there rain gutters? Sewers?
10. Are any municipal off-site improvements needed or being made? If so, will the cost of these improvements be billed to the subject property?
11. Is street parking adequate for current and projected needs?
12. Is the site affected by any locational obsolescence such as an undesirable view, noise, or fumes?
13. Is there any evidence of soil slippage or erosion?

Local zoning and building codes also have a very great impact on the site and will be discussed further on in this chapter. You should also determine whether the subject site is located in a flood hazard area. Flood hazard areas are designated by the Federal Emergency Management Agency and are shown on their Flood Insurance Rate Maps (available from the Agency or the city's planning department). Federally regulated mortgage lenders require flood insurance for properties located in these areas, and the lender usually relies on the appraiser for this information.

ESTIMATING THE QUALITY OF THE IMPROVEMENTS

Any appraisal requires that you form an opinion as to the quality of the improvements (i.e., the apartment building[s]) on the site. Readily observable telltale signs of quality levels include:

1. *Quality of Workmanship*. Look for haphazardly completed improvements that evidence little pride of workmanship.

2. *Roof*. Short eaves protrusions, little roof pitch, and poor quality materials are evidence of poor construction quality.

3. *Building Contours*. Inexpensively constructed buildings usually have relatively flat exterior walls with few contours along their sides.

4. *Trim and Decoration*. Buildings of poor quality will exhibit little expense for trim and decoration.

5. *Kitchen and Bath Fixtures.* Finishing touches such as real ceramic tile and drawers on rollers are evidence of good quality construction. The quality of kitchen and bath cabinetry is almost always consistent with the remainder of the building.

6. *Amenities.* Poor quality buildings will usually not have amenities such as fireplaces or extra-high ceilings. The amount of common area amenities can also be items you use in making your determination.

7. *Heating/Cooling.* Depending on climate, different geographic locations have differing standards as to what constitutes good or poor quality heating and cooling systems.

Nowadays, the use of plaster interior walls in new construction is almost non-existent—almost all apartments are built with drywall, regardless of overall building quality. Doors, exterior walls, and window frames provide indications of quality, but again are subject to differing standards depending on climate and product availability.

The *Residential Cost Handbook,* published by Marshall and Swift Company (Los Angeles), provides pictures and written descriptions of their quality ratings, which are "Fair," "Average," "Good," "Very Good," and "Excellent."

MEASURING AND ROOM COUNTS

Most lenders require a sketch of the building as well as each of the floorplans. If available, the property's construction blueprints can be reduced to a size that will conveniently fit in the report. This can be done by a blueprint shop. If plans are not available, use legal-size graph paper for your sketches.

Figure 2.2 shows a typical building sketch. Note that directional orientation, dimensions, and area calculations are provided. While trade groups have standardized the measuring techniques for office and retail spaces, this has not happened for apartments (except in New York). The gross square footage measurement for an apartment building is generally considered to consist of the floor area, inclusive of walls, interior hallways, stairways, and lobbies. Items that might be excluded (or provided for in a different measurement figure) are garages, basements, and patios. If an area is questionable for inclusion, the test is usually whether the same square foot base cost as used in the cost approach would be applied to the item.

Figure 2.3 shows a typical floorplan sketch. Note that the rooms and dividing walls are identified. The square footage measurement consists of the rentable area, which is exclusive of the perimeter walls.

Room counts, as they appear in the FHLMC/FNMA appraisal forms, are somewhat unconventional. The rent schedule on page 5 of Form 71A calls for three figures: total rooms, bedrooms, and baths. Total rooms includes living rooms, kitchens, dens, bedrooms, and separate dining rooms. Service porches, hallways,

SKETCH ADDENDUM

Borrower/Client
Property Address
City County State Zip Code
Lender

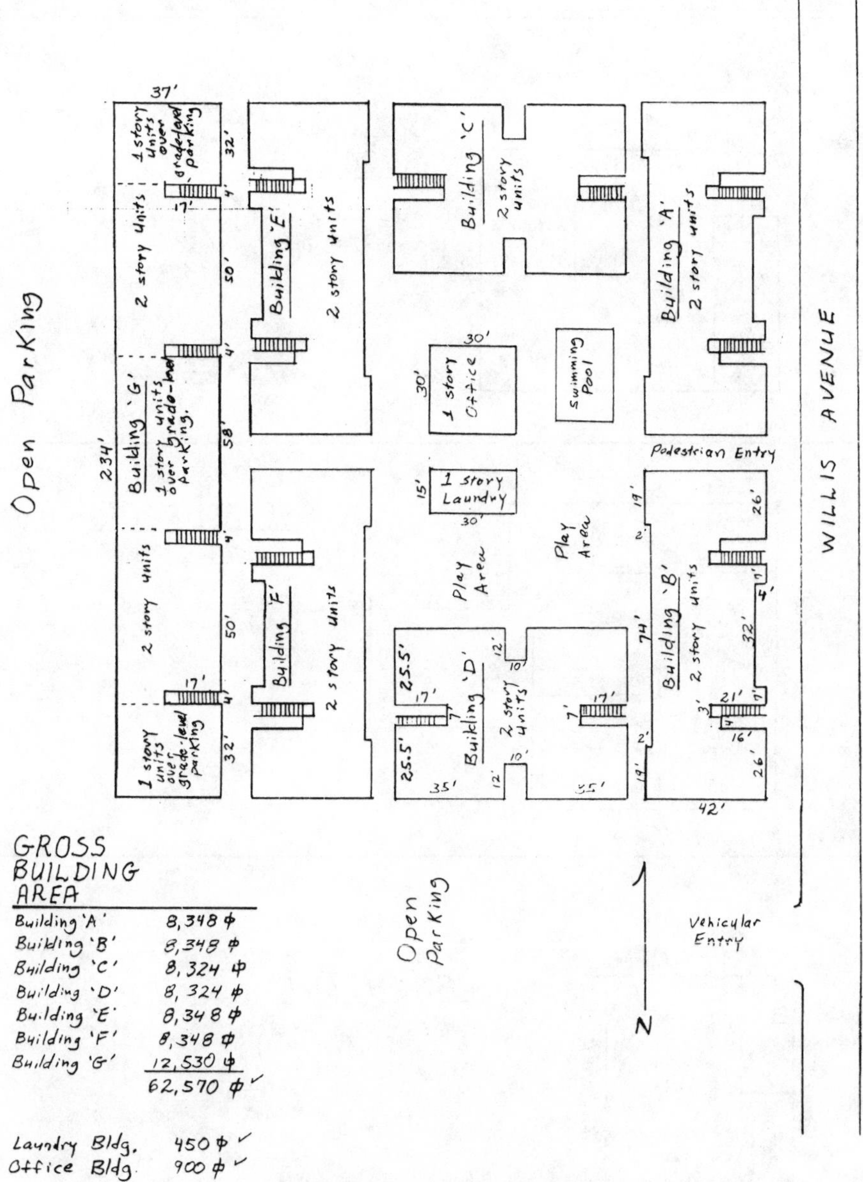

Figure 2.2. Building Sketch

SKETCH ADDENDUM

Borrower/Client			
Property Address			
City	County	State	Zip Code
Lender			

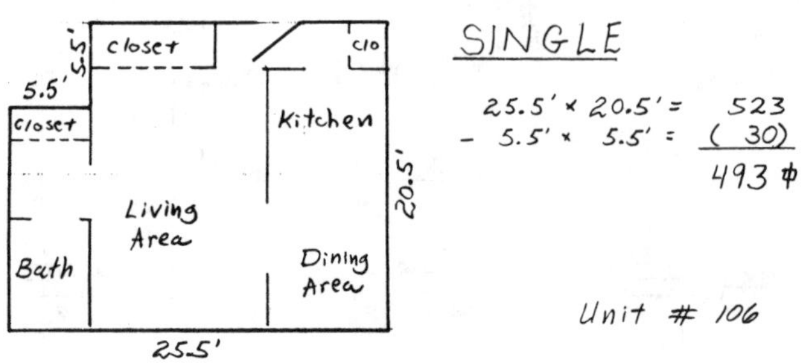

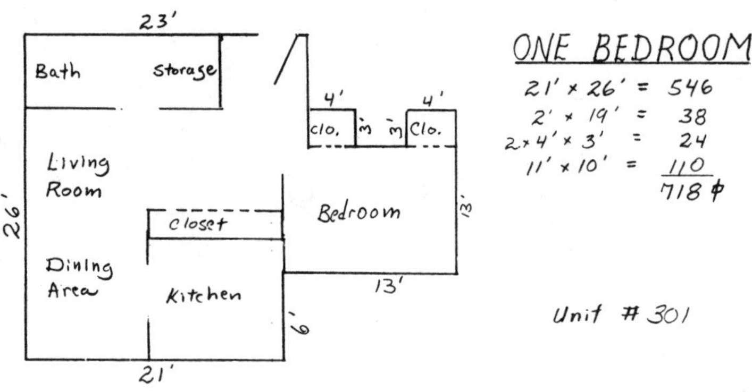

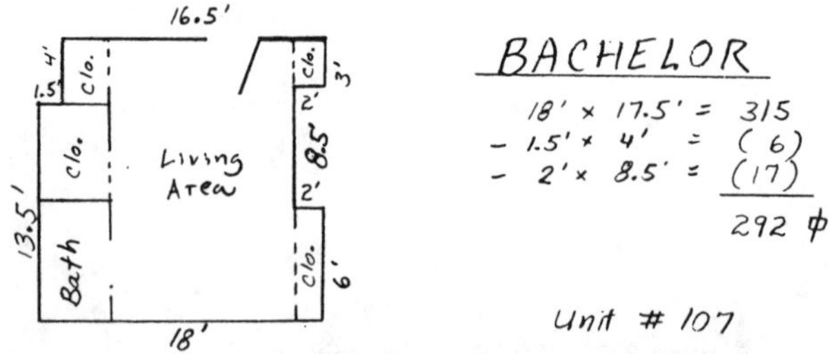

Figure 2.3. Floorplan Sketch

balconies, patios, and bathrooms are not included. A one-bedroom, one-bath apartment is designated on the form as having 3-1-1 rooms. A two-bedroom, one-bath unit is designated as 4-2-1. A three-quarter bath has a stand-up shower rather than a tub. A half-bath has a toilet and wash basin but no shower or bathing facilities.

Depending on local terminology, a studio unit is a unit with either two stories or a unit without a bedroom. As a unit without a separate bedroom, a studio is designated on the form as a 2-0-1. This is also the definition of a single unit. A bachelor unit does not have kitchen facilities and is designated as 1-0-1.

REPORTING YOUR FINDINGS

Figure 2.4 depicts the completed lower portion of page 1 of the appraisal report for our case study. The narrative description at the bottom provides a quick summary of the property and notes any item which a lender or investor might well perceive as being very important—in this case, the property is in need of a new roof. Note that the report includes the appraiser's estimated cost of the replacement and some indication as to whether any damage has been caused by this situation. Items that you specially note may include health and safety hazards, uncompleted construction or renovation work, master-metered utilities, mismanagement, etc.

A completed page 3 of the form, which describes site and improvements, can be seen as Figure 2.1. Any unusual or important aspects of the property have been emphasized here, as well.

Any items which might raise a question or concern on the part of the reader should be fully addressed. These include items needing repair or replacement, health or safety problems, inadequate parking, negative influences from adjacent land usages, etc. After reporting the problem and perhaps including a photograph of it in the report, you should provide the following conclusions where applicable:

1. Can the problem be fixed? What is your recommendation for dealing with the problem?
2. What is the cost of fixing the problem?
3. Is the problem having an effect on tenancy?
4. Is the marketability of the property impaired due to this problem? If so, to what degree?

Where applicable, you should state whether you consider the seriousness of the problem to be of no, little, moderate, or serious adverse effect.

Further on in this chapter is a list of items you should note during your appraisal. The following can be of special importance and deserve additional discussion.

```
Subject property has good tenant and ownership appeal. The neighborhood is
considered average for the city. Current management is considered appropriate
for the subject's continued operation. Tenancy is of average desirability.
Management states that the building usually operates at 94% to 98% occupancy.
Roof needs replacement (see Photos Nos. 21 and 22); estimated cost is $8,000
to $10,000. No apparent water damage.
```

FHLMC Form 71A Rev. 8/77 Page 1 of 8 FNMA Form 1050 12/83

Figure 2.4. Lower part of page 1, 71A Form

Roof Inspection

Roofs are not only costly to replace but can allow severe water damage as well. Almost any building over two stories high will have a stairway leading to the roof. When possible, always inspect the roof and take photographs. Note the age of the roof and what repairs have been made. Types of roofs common to apartment buildings are:

1. *Asphalt shingle.* Usually the easiest to inspect; presents the least problems.
2. *Flat root with mineral cap sheet.* Mineral cap sheet roofing is identified by its light-colored granular surface and many seams (it is manufactured in narrow rolls).
3. *Flat roof with built-up surface.* This roof is characterized by its gravel surface (which deflects the sun's rays from the underlying emulsion).

Gravel roofs are the most difficult to inspect because they hide defects. Actually, the term "flat roof" is usually a misnomer; almost all roofs will have a slight slope of at least ⅛″ per foot to facilitate drainage.

The following items should be kept in mind while inspecting roofs:

1. *Ceiling stains.* Roofs must be inspected from underneath as well as from overhead.
2. *Ponded water.* Discolored areas are evidence of improper drainage slopes (Fig. 2.5).
3. *Penetrations.* Penetrations through the roofing membrane for vent pipes, air conditioning units, signs, TV antennas, etc. are likely spots for roof leaks. These areas should be well sealed.
4. *Sheet metal flashings.* Metal flashings (used to seal the edges of the roof membrane) have a high coefficient of expansion and contraction, often causing cracks where they join the roof membrane.
5. *Blisters.* Blisters are the delamination between the various layers of roofing and are usually the result of heated moisture underneath the top surface. Extreme cases can show evidence of ponding between the blisters.

Figure 2.5 Water ponding, as is seen in the reflected images of the vents, is caused by roof's improper drainage slope.

Typical life expectancies are as follows:

Asphalt shingle, 230 lb.	15–20 years
Mineral cap sheet	10–15 years
Built-up with gravel	10–12 years
Cedar shingles	10–15 years

Decking and Walkways

Two- or three-story buildings with exterior entries (as opposed to hallway entries) generally have unit access from elevated walkways built along the side of the building. The surfaces of these walkways or decks are prone to deterioration and should be maintained in good condition.

Walkway or decking surfaces of older buildings generally consist of magnesite (a light-weight concrete made of a magnesium carbonate compound). Newer buildings more often have a resin and Fiberglas ("elastonomeric") surface which is usually identified by its non-slip granular finish. Both types of surfaces are applied over a plywood substructure and are prone to cracks and subsequent penetration by water. Like roof leaks, they are not always visible to the naked eye. Such penetration is evidenced by paint pealing, swelling of the surfaces, leaks into apartments, and water stains under the decks.

Another problem is the wearing through of the glossy magnesite surface, exposing the porous subsurface. Both magnesite and elastonomeric materials have little elasticity and tend to crack around the penetration of metal railings and post assemblies. The wood substructure can consequently dryrot and repair work can be very expensive. Rooflines should extend beyond these walkways. Patios and balconies constructed of these materials can cause problems as well.

Compliance with Building Codes

Most pre-1960 properties I appraise do not comply with current building codes. Obviously, an owner can incur disastrous financial consequences when a city requires that a property be brought to code. Less obvious is the effect on financing availability, and consequently on value, because of lenders' policies regarding such requirements. Common cases of non-compliance are as follows:

1. The property does not provide enough parking.
2. The existing apartment building has more units than would be allowed if the site were to be redeveloped today.
3. The building does not conform to requirements regarding potential hazards, including earthquake and fire safety.

Buildings subject to the first two cases are often considered by cities as being "permitted non-conforming uses": Continued use of the property is permitted even though it does not conform to current codes. Despite this status, lenders often require insurance for a possible situation in which the building is partially or wholly destroyed and the city requires any replacement to conform to current code.

While they usually tolerate the continued existence of certain inadequacies, cities often require that health and safety violations be corrected. For example, the city of Los Angeles requires all pre-1934 unreinforced masonry bearing-wall buildings to undergo strengthening work (Fig. 2.6). The cost is usually between $7 to $15 per square foot! In addition, all pre-1943 apartment buildings three or more stories high are required to be fitted with alarms, sprinkler systems (Fig. 2.7), stairway shaft enclosures, and special doors. Each of these ordinances has affected hundreds of buildings within the city. Values of pre-compliance buildings are typi-

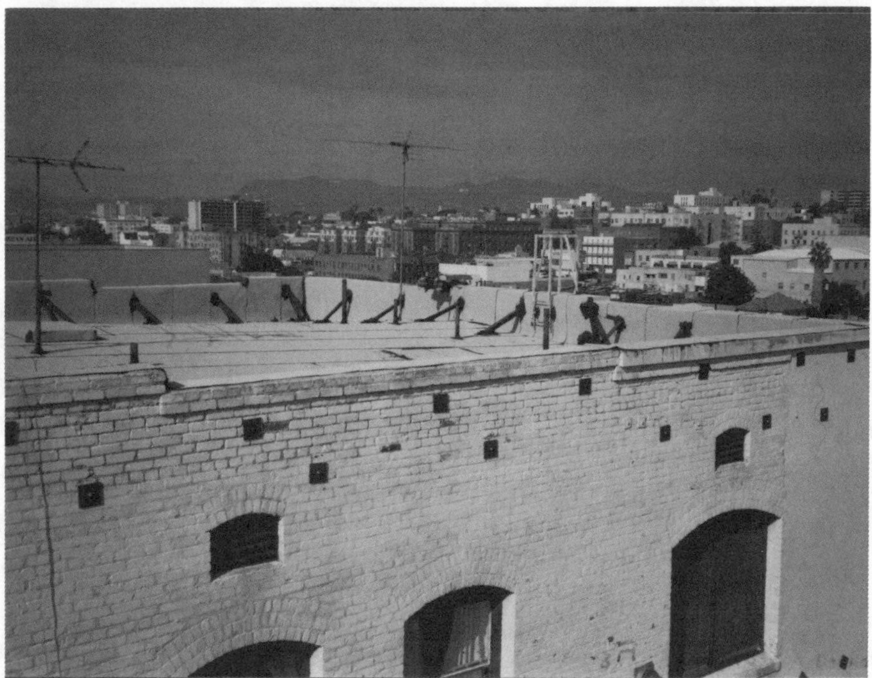

Figure 2.6 Metal plates along the brick walls and the steel the parapets were braces for the parapets were retrofitted to bring this older building into compliance with its city's structural safety ordinance.

cally $8,000 to $10,000 per unit less than those which have been brought to code compliance. An appraiser's unawareness of such ordinances or inaccurate reporting is an open door to errors-and-omissions law suits.

Elevators

Any building over two stories generally has at least one elevator. Buildings from two to four stories most often have a hydraulic elevator which operates by oil pumped into and out of a hydraulic plunger cylinder, much the same as a grease rack in a service station bay. The mechanics for this type of installation are located adjacent to the bottom of the shaft. Hydraulic elevators cost substantially less to maintain than electric elevators. The latter are more suitable for building heights over 60 feet and requiring five or more stops. Doors, controls, and other cab appointments can be identical in both types of elevators. Note the appearance of the cab. Is it appealing?

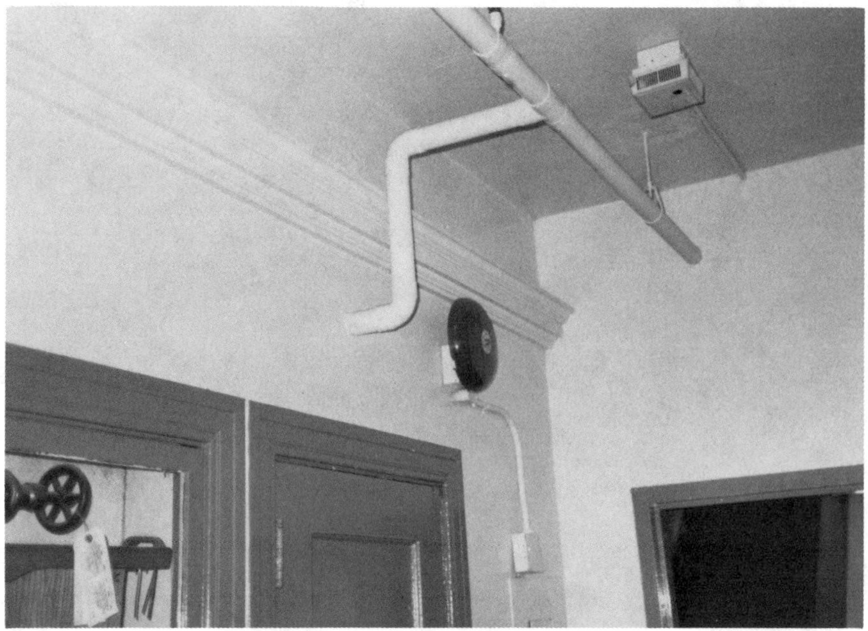

Figure 2.7 Retrofitted alarms and sprinkler system in this older building are required by its city's recent fire-safety ordinances.

Elevators should have a service contract that can be a preventative maintenance (oil and grease) or, preferably, a full service (including labor and parts) agreement. The complexities of the elevator shaft and mechanics make a thorough inspection practically impossible, but they should still be checked for any obvious problems.

Water Heaters

Investors most often prefer buildings with individual water heaters because the gas consumption is usually billed to the tenant. Gas water heaters should be in a vented enclosure and can usually be found quite easily. Electric water heaters are generally short in height and are often inconspicuously placed in a lower kitchen cupboard adjacent to the sink. Twenty-gallon heaters are sufficient for single units (units with kitchens but no bedrooms), but larger units should have water heaters with at least a 30-gallon capacity. Inquire as to how many of the water heaters are typically replaced over the course of a year.

Central water heaters are usually mounted in the basement or a separate room, but may also be located on the roof, outside in a fenced area, or in the laundry room. These heaters often have circulating pumps which keep the hot water continuously circulating through a loop which travels the building, thereby reducing the time it takes to provide hot water to the tap. These pumps are occasionally controlled by timers, in order to limit the electrical usage during low demand hours.

The operating capacity of a water heater will be given on a tag on its side and is measured in number of gallons and BTU output. Check to see if the system has a water softener, filter, purifier, or chemical feeder. Although the installation of such devices implies that they are necessary, they can be costly to maintain and operate. Central hot water systems commonly have heater tanks with a 100-gallon capacity. Tanks of the same size may have substantially different replacement costs due to the type of ignition and the differences in BTU ratings.

Asbestos

Various diseases have been linked to the presence of airborne asbestos. The United States Environmental Protection Agency estimates that approximately 765,000 public and commercial buildings contain asbestos materials. The presence of asbestos-containing material (ACM) does not necessarily endanger a building's occupants—exposure is unlikely as long as the material remains in good condition and is not disturbed. However, a renovation or maintenance project could release asbestos fibers and create a potential hazard.

Asbestos in buildings is found in three forms:

1. Sprayed or troweled on ceilings and walls (surfacing material). A good example of this is a ceiling sprayed with acoustical plaster.
2. Insulation around hot or cold pipes, ducts, boilers, and tanks.
3. In a variety of other products such as ceiling and floor tiles and wallboards.

In general, the first two categories cause the greatest concern, especially if the material is friable. (Friable material can be crumbled, pulverized, or reduced to powder by hand pressure.) Asbestos problems are usually remedied by removal, enclosure, or encapsulation.

Aside from merely checking building records (which may or may not provide accurate evidence of ACM), identifying asbestos is difficult and is a job for a qualified laboratory. Most of the asbestos I see in apartment buildings is used for insulating hot water heaters and pipes. In one extreme example, my appraisal assignment on a 1960s high-rise apartment building was quickly canceled after the lender was notified that the property needed two million dollars of asbestos correction work. Typically, levels of asbestos in buildings containing ACM are 10,000 to 100,000 times lower than levels in asbestos industry workplaces where asbestos-related diseases have been documented. However, lending institutions are showing concern, and one lender I deal with states in its appraisal guidelines that it is the appraiser's responsibility to denote whether the property contains asbestos. This is an impractical requirement for most assignments. I state in the limiting conditions of every one of my appraisals that such identification is not within the scope of the assignment, that I've assumed that no such materials are present, that I take no responsibility if they are present, and that I urge the client to obtain the services of an expert in this field.

RESEARCHING PUBLIC RECORDS

Availability of public records varies greatly from one municipality to another. However, the following items, many of which are needed for the completion of an appraisal, are often located at either city or county offices.

1. Zoning requirements for the property
2. Legal or assessor's parcel map
3. Flood hazard maps
4. Availability of utilities
5. Cost of business license
6. Recent building permits (Applications for permits of other apartment buildings are also helpful in researching land sales and projecting the number of new units to be constructed)
7. Sales of apartment buildings
8. Recorded transfer documents for verifying comparable sales
9. Property tax and assessment data
10. Building permits
11. Nearby development which will positively or adversely affect the subject property

CHECKLIST AND QUESTIONS

You should insist that the property manager or owner accompany you on your inspection. The following details should be observed and reported. In addition, it seems as though every property is affected by some unusual influence—be it location, building obsolescence, condition, etc. These items and their impact on income and/or value should be fully addressed in the appraisal report. Where applicable, you should note the quality, condition, and adequacy of an item.

RENTS AND OCCUPANCY

1. What is the current occupancy?
2. What is the typical occupancy?
3. Which units are currently vacant? (get unit numbers)
4. Why are these units vacant? (typical vacancy, asking rents too high, bad market, repairs)
5. What are the asking rents for the various types of units? Does the manager or owner consider these to conform to the market level?
6. Are any rent concessions being offered?

TENANCY

1. How are prospective tenants screened?
2. What types of jobs do the tenants hold?
3. How many have cars? Is parking adequate?
4. How many children are there in the complex?
5. What are the ages of the children?
6. How many evictions are there per year?
7. How many tenancy changes (turnovers) are there on an annual or monthly basis?

MANAGEMENT

1. What constitutes the on-site management and maintenance staff?
2. How are vacant units marketed?
3. What is the appearance of the rental office?
4. What are the responsibilities of the on-site management?
5. What constitutes off-site management?
6. What are the responsibilities of the off-site management?
7. How long have the on- and off-site management groups been running the property?

SITE

1. Are there any easements or encroachments?
2. Is drainage adequate?
3. What is the topography?
4. Does the parcel map conform to what actually exists?

5. Is there any exposure to hazards or nuisances?
6. What is the vehicular ingress and egress?
7. Is there a fire hydrant nearby?
8. Is the site serviced with the necessary utilities (telephone, gas, electricity, water, sewer)?
9. Are curbs and sidewalks installed?
10. Does the surrounding area (including streets and alleys) provide for the drainage of run-off water?
11. Are there street lights?
12. In what condition are the site improvements?

COMMON AREA

1. What is in the landscape?
2. Are there built-in sprinklers?
3. Are the sprinklers automatic?
4. Are the walkways adequate?
5. How many parking spaces are there?
6. Are the parking and pedestrian entries secured?
7. Is there adequate lighting?
8. Are there any recreational facilities?
9. Are there adequate laundry facilities?
10. Are the utility meters and electrical lines well protected?
11. Is the rubbish area well shielded?
12. Is the rubbish area conveniently located for both the tenants and the disposal service?
13. What is the condition of the parking area surfacing (Fig. 2.8)?
14. If trash bins are used, are they on a concrete pad? (Asphalt can be destroyed quickly.)
15. Have stairs and decks been maintained continually to prevent dryrot of the substructure?
16. Is the pool heated? If so, for how many months of the year? Does it need an acid wash? Is it fenced? Are the proper warnings to swimmers in place? Is the pool surface or deck cracked?

BUILDING EXTERIOR

1. Of what materials are the walls constructed?
2. What is the roofing material?

Figure 2.8 Asphalt cracks in parking area create water ponding and further deterioration.

3. Is roof drainage adequate?
4. What is the condition of the windows and screens? Are any missing?
5. Is the entry attractive?
6. In what condition are the mail boxes?
7. Are there security systems? Do they work properly?
8. What is the condition of the paint? The walls (Fig. 2.9)?

BUILDING INTERIOR

1. Make a diagram of the units.
2. What built-in appliances are in the kitchen?
3. What free-standing appliances belong to the building?
4. What type of heating system is there?
5. What type of air conditioning system is there?
6. Are there individual thermostats?

Figure 2.9 The pattern of these cracks and the outward bulge in the wall indicate a possibly serious structural problem.

7. Is there adequate ventilation in the kitchens and baths?
8. What are the floor coverings?
9. What do the drapes or other window coverings consist of?
10. Is storage adequate?
11. Are the units wired for cable TV? Is this supplied free or must the tenant pay a subscription fee?
12. What do the kitchen and bath fixtures consist of?
13. Do wiring and plumbing appear properly done?
14. Check the water pressure.
15. Are there circuit breakers or fuses?
16. Are the doors and windows adequately secured? Do they operate properly?
17. Is the property in compliance with the applicable building codes, especially those relating to fire and safety?

18. Are there any fireplaces? Do they have a gas log? If wood-burning, does the flue work properly?
19. Are the paint colors pleasant? Will they coordinate with a variety of furnishing tastes?
20. Are the appliances operating properly?
21. Do the shower and sink drain properly?
22. Are unit interiors affected by any persistent outside noise?
23. What preparation work does management usually do for new rentals?

RENOVATION POTENTIAL

Many investors specialize in renovating properties with upside potential. Their criteria are simple: The property's value after renovation should be worth more than the cost of the property plus the renovation expenses, and the profit should be sufficient to cover the investor's risk and time investment. The appraiser should recognize such a property and consider whether it should be producing more income in its present state, how management and tenancy changes can upgrade the property, and what the costs of turn-around would be.

RETIREMENT HOUSING

The supply is low in comparison to projected demand, and retirement housing developments are becoming more prevalent. This type of property has several distinguishing features:

1. Any building with two or more stories should have an elevator.
2. Parking requirements are fewer than for typical apartment buildings. As an incentive to build retirement apartments, cities may grant additional density allowances and require fewer parking spaces.
3. Additional recreational and security amenities are generally favored.
4. More emphasis is placed on units being equipped for the handicapped, including grab bars in the bathrooms.
5. The staff may require substantial space and facilities.
6. Meal facilities may be included.

Facilities and services cover a wide range. Construction cost is often higher, and these projects typically take much longer to achieve stabilized occupancy. Appraising buildings with staffs or meal services is beyond the scope of this book.

BUYER'S FREQUENT OBJECTIONS

The following is a partial list of concerns often voiced by purchasers:

1. Poor overall condition
2. Undesirable tenancy
3. Master-metered utilities
4. No built-in landscape sprinklers
5. Window mechanisms requiring too much expense to bring to working condition and keep operational (especially with double-hung windows)
6. Poor drainage in parking area
7. Poor roof drainage
8. Short remaining life of replacement items such as air conditioners, carpets, drapes
9. Unsatisfactory condition of nearby properties
10. Insufficient parking
11. Requirements for compliance with health and safety codes
12. Landscaping requiring intensive maintenance
13. Persistent maintenance problems, especially with the plumbing system

This is not a complete list but it does provide an idea of items which affect a property's marketability. It should be noted that some buyers see these conditions as opportunities.

CHAPTER THREE

THE RENT ROLL

The appraiser must have a rent roll for any existing property being appraised. It should accurately reflect the rents as of the date of the appraisal, as well as contain a notation as to which units are occupied and which are vacant. The four items that must appear on the rent roll are the unit number, room count, rental amount and identification of vacant units.

Figure 3.1 shows a carelessly prepared rent roll actually submitted by an owner. Items missing include the room count for each unit, the date of the rent roll, and the source of the information. Also, no explanation is given as to why there are two columns of rental figures (upon investigation, the owner said that the right-hand column contained the proposed rents for a later date).

On the other hand, Figure 3.2 shows an owner-supplied rent roll that is much easier to work with. Note that while the owner included square footage figures in the Figure 3.2 rent roll, the units were remeasured and found to be slightly smaller.

REVIEWING THE RENT ROLL

While the owner would most often benefit by reporting a higher income, the accuracy of the rent roll is always checked by doing a rent survey, which is discussed in Chapter 4. You should also verify rents with a few of the tenants. Rent rolls sometimes show vacant units as receiving the market rental rate without specifying in any way that the unit is vacant—be sure to ask the right questions. Know and report the term of the rental agreement (e.g., month to month, one year, etc.). Obtaining and reviewing copies of the actual rental agreements is advisable. Also, be sure to review the contract and ask the owner or manager whether the listed rents

rent roll

Date	"Always Date and Initial Your Remarks"			Initials
	#1 Winberry	$ 520	July 1st	$ 560
	#2 Castro	$ 400		440
	#3 Santillean	$ 480		525
	#4 Nguyen	$ 480		525
	#5 Sloan	$ 480		525
	#6 King	$ 480		525
	#7 Verbch	$ 400		440
	#8 Izquerdo	$ 400		440
	#9 Orozco	$ 400		440
	#10 Mendoza	$ 480		525
	#11 Swett	$ 520		560
	#12 Armstrong	$ 400		440
	#13A Colchado	$ 480		525
	#14 Modarelli	$ 480		525
	#15 Fierro	$ 480		525
	#16 Ortiz	$ 480		525
	#17 Landeros	$ 520		560
	#18 Salazar	$ 480		525
	#19 Nguyen	$ 520		560
	#20 Fernandez	$ 400		440
	#21 Salazar	$ 440		440
	#22 Catoni	$ 480		525
		$ 10,200		$ 11,095
	Laundry $ 200 per month			

Figure 3.1. Carelessly prepared owner's rent roll

RENT SCHEDULE
8/4/86

UNIT	NAME	RENT	SQUARE FEET	BDRM BATHS	L=LOWER U=UPPER
1	Aguilar	470	765	2-1	L
2	Amezuca	400	560	1-1	L
3	Rented as of 9/1/86	400	560	1-1	L
4	R. Pacheco	385	560	1-1	L
5		400	560	1-1	L
6	Martinez	495	756	2-1	L
7	Rented as of 9/1/86	400	513	1-1	L
8	Martha Luna,Mgr.	495	756	2-1	L
9	T. Allen	495	756	2-1	L
10	Arrieta	495	756	2-1	L
11	Rodriguez	495	756	2-1	L
12	Benitez	495	756	2-1	L
14	Aceves	526	756	2-1	L
15	Onate	503	756	2-1	L
16	Ruiz	400	560	1-1	L
17	A. Aparicio	400	560	1-1	U
18	Gurrola	429	560	1-1	U
19	Vargas	400	560	1-1	U
20	Rosario pacheco	513	756	2-1	U
21	Ruiz	400	513	1-1	U
22	Ruiz	400	656	1-1	U
23	Diego	492	756	2-1	U
24	Mercado	400	656	1-1	U
25	Gurrola	520	756	2-1	U
26	Munoz	492	756	2-1	U
27	Fernandez	530	756	2-1	U
28	Carlos Perdomo	495	756	2-1	U
29	Jil	492	756	2-1	U
30	Rosa Mroales	492	756	2-1	U
31	Rodriguez	425	360	1-1	U
		$13,734	20,030		

Figure 3.2. Well-prepared owner's rent roll

reflect any rental concessions (e.g., owner providing one month free rent for the tenant signing a one-year lease).

Do the rental figures reflect just the amount paid for the unit, or do they include any personal property rental as well? Because they are lending only on the real property (exclusive of personal property), many lenders will not lend on personal property such as furniture or free-standing kitchen appliances. If the rent reflects personal property, you may wish to reduce the rental figures accordingly or, alternatively, deduct the depreciated value of the personal property from the final value estimate. The first option, reducing income, can often result in a corresponding reduction in value which exceeds the value of the personal property—the lender may specify which method to use.

Income from miscellaneous sources should also be included. Consistency is important here. At least in the market approach, the miscellaneous income should be of the same categories as reflected in the comparables' gross income. Wanting high appraisals, borrowers are occasionally adamant about including forfeited deposits. However, the income figures from virtually all comparables omit this type of income, and it would be unfair to include it for the subject property.

The only income from miscellaneous sources which is generally included in appraisals is that from the parking, extra storage and laundry room usage. One might argue that laundry room income emanates from personal property and, like income from free-standing kitchen appliances, should be omitted from the appraisal. In that case, you might treat any building-owned laundry machines as though they were owned by a service company and provided to the apartment building under a revenue-sharing agreement. The revenue split is commonly 50/50. Hence, the total laundry income is projected and the building is accorded 50 percent of this amount. In any case, laundry income is often reflected in the comparables' gross income figures and must be included in order to make fair comparisons in the valuation process.

While the Figure 3.2 rent roll indicates a total of 31 units, there are actually only 30 units. As is frequently the case, unit number 13 has been omitted in order to put any superstitious tenants at ease. Even the Figure 3.1 rent roll shows the unit that would ordinarily be designated unit number 13 has been numbered unit 12A. Beware of this situation when counting the number of units on the property.

REDRAWING THE RENT ROLL

Figure 3.3 is an appraiser's revised version of the Figure 3.1 rent roll. Note the additional information included by the appraiser. If you wish to include a number of items (such as which units have balconies, views, etc.), it may be appropriate to include a column with numbered or alphabetical codes that are explained in a foot-

213 S. Willson Avenue, Metropolis
October 29, 1987

Unit No.	Vacant/ Occupied	Unit Type	Rentable Sq. Ft.	Current Actual Monthly Rent	Current Market Monthly Rent
1	Occupied	2-1	710	$ 520	$ 540
2	Occupied	Single	385	$ 400	$ 440
3	Occupied	1-1	588	$ 480	$ 500
4	Occupied	1-1	588	$ 480	$ 500
5	Occupied	1-1	588	$ 480	$ 500
6	Occupied	1-1	588	$ 480	$ 500
7	Occupied	Single	385	$ 400	$ 440
8	Occupied	Single	385	$ 400	$ 440
9	Occupied	Single	385	$ 400	$ 440
10	Occupied	2-1	710	$ 480	$ 540
11	Occupied	2-1	710	$ 520	$ 540
12	Occupied	Single	385	$ 400	$ 440
12a	Occupied	1-1	588	$ 480	$ 500
14	Occupied	1-1	588	$ 480	$ 500
15	Occupied	1-1	588	$ 480	$ 500
16	Occupied	1-1	588	$ 480	$ 500
17	Occupied	2-1	710	$ 520	$ 540
18	Occupied	1-1	588	$ 480	$ 500
19	Occupied	2-1	710	$ 520	$ 540
20	Occupied	Single	385	$ 400	$ 440
21	Occupied	Single	385	$ 440	$ 440
22	Occupied	1-1	588	$ 480	$ 500
				$10,200	$10,780

NOTES:

1. Market rent is: $440 single
   $500 1-1
   $540 2-1
2. All rental agreements are on a month-to-month basis.
3. Total actual rents are 5.4% below total market rents.
4. Actual figures are identical to those listed on the owner-supplied rent roll which is seen on the following page.

Figure 3.3. Appraiser's revised rent roll

COMPARABLE RENTAL DATA

Comparables selected are the most recent rentals, similar and proximate, known to the undersigned, that a tenant of subject property would have given consideration to renting.

ITEM	COMPARABLE No. 1	COMPARABLE No. 2	COMPARABLE No. 3
Address	1052 Franklin Avenue Metropolis	948 Franklin Avenue Metropolis	1112 Hightower Boulevard Metropolis
Proximity to subj.	3 blocks west	2 blocks west	4 blocks north
Map Code	78-F4	78-F4	78-E5
Date of rental survey	10-29-88	10-29-88	10-29-88
Brief description of property improvements	No. Units 54 No. Vac. 2 Yr. Blt. 69 3-story stucco over sub. garage. Pool. Full security. Centercourt.	No. Units 78 No. Vac. 2 Yr. Blt. 72 3-story stucco over sub. garage. Pool. Full security. Centercourt.	No. Units 35 No. Vac. 3 Yr. Blt. 70 4-story stucco over sub. garage. Pool. Full security. Centercourt.
Quality & condition	Quality Average Condition Average-	Quality Average Condition Average+	Quality Average Condition Average+

Individual unit breakdown

	Comp. No. 1 Tot.	BR	b	Size Sq. Ft.	Monthly Rent $	per sq. ft.	Comp. No. 2 Tot.	BR	b	Size Sq. Ft.	Monthly Rent $	per sq. ft.	Comp. No. 3 Tot.	BR	b	Size Sq. Ft.	Monthly Rent $	per sq. ft.
	3	1	1	650	660	102 ¢	3	1	1	684	685	100 ¢	3	1	1	650	690	106 ¢
	4	2	2	850	755	89 ¢	4	2	2	842	790	94 ¢	3	1	1	650	700	108 ¢
													4	2	2	850	800	94 ¢
													4	2	2	850	810	95 ¢

Comparable No. 1: Includes one parking space. Additional parking @ $20/ space.

Comparable No. 2: Includes one parking space with 1 BR, 2 spaces for 2 BR.

Comparable No. 3: $700 1 BR and $810 2 BR are corner units.

ITEM	COMPARABLE No. 1	COMPARABLE No. 2	COMPARABLE No. 3
Utilities, furniture and amenities included in rent	C & H water. Unfurnished. Small balcony. Built-in range. No DW.	C & H water. Unfurnished. Small balcony. Built-in range, DW.	C & H water. Unfurnished. Large balcony. Built-in range, DW. 1 pkg. space for 1BR, 2 spaces for 2BR.
Comparison to subject	Location: Similar	Similar	Similar
	Quality: Similar	Similar	Similar
	Condition: Inferior	Similar	Similar
	Amenities: Similar	Similar	Similar
	Ten. Appeal: Inferior	Similar	Superior
	Less appealing design and landscape.		

General comments (including any rental concessions) if applicable: No rent concessions. Comps ordered from least to most expensive. Subject is most similar to No. 2. All rents on a month-to-month basis. All comps have tenancies and management similar to the subject. Comps show a 4.2% vacancy rate.

MONTHLY RENT SCHEDULE – SUBJECT PROPERTY

Rental schedule is shown by type of units. Scheduled rents are actual rentals for an existing property, or projected rents for a proposed or incomplete building. Economic rents are forecasted rents to indicate the fair market rental the subject units would command if available for rent on the open market.

No. of Units	Unit Rm. Count Tot.	BR	b	Total Rooms	Sq. Ft. Area Per Unit	No. Units Vacant	SCHEDULED RENTS Per Unit Unfurn.	Furn.	Total Rents	ECONOMIC RENTS Per Unit Unfurn.	Furn.	Total Rents	Per Sq. Ft.	or Room
11	3	1	1	33	670	0	$ 660–680	$	$ 7,455	$ 685	$	$ 7,535	102 ¢	$ 228
11	3	1	1	33	695	0	650–670		7,360	675		7,425	97	225
14	4	2	2	56	865	0	755–800		11,060	800		11,200	92	200
14	4	2	2	56	890	0	750–790		10,950	790		11,060	89	198
	See below for explanation of price ranges.													
50	◄ TOTAL ►			178		0			$36,825			$ 37,220		

OTHER MONTHLY INCOME

	Scheduled	Economic
Parking	$ 0	$ 0
Laundry Income @ $4.00/unit/month	$ 200	$ 200
Commercial Space	$	$
	$	$
	$	$
Total Gross Monthly Income	$ 37,025	$ 37,420
Total Gross Annual Income	$ 444,300	$ 449,040

Utilities included in scheduled (actual) rents: [X] Water [ ] Gas [ ] Heat [ ] Electric [ ] Air Conditioning [X] Hot water

Utilities included in economic rents: [X] Water [ ] Gas [ ] Heat [ ] Electric [ ] Air Conditioning [X] Hot water

If proposed project or project under construction, the rent up time necessary, after completion, to lease 80% of the units at the projected economic rents is estimated to be N/A months.

Comments (including any rental concessions in scheduled rents, or anticipated in economic rents; if none, so state). See Addendum for current rent roll. Scheduled rents verified with resident manager. No rent concessions for subject. All tenants are on month-to-month agreements. Actual and economic rents reflect one parking space per 1BR, two spaces per 2BR. Current asking rents are $680 for 670SF 1BR units facing centercourt, $670 for 695SF 1BR facing outside, $800 for 865 2BR units facing centercourt, $790 for 890SF units facing outside. Based on rent survey discussion with resident manager, asking rents appear to be at economic level. Scheduled rents are 1.1% below estimated economic level. No personal property included in rents.

Figure 3.4. 71A Form, Page 5

OCEAN VIEW 2 BEDROOM

UNIT #	EXPOSURE	SCHED.RENT(ASKING)	ECON.RENT	RENT DATE
133	WEST	1,300	1,300	8/85
134	WEST	1,290	1,300	12/84
135	WEST	1,245	1,300	2/85
136	WEST	1,245	1,300	10/82
233	WEST	1,245	1,300	12/78
234	WEST	1,390	1,300	4/86
235	WEST	1,245	1,300	9/83
236	WEST	1,280	1,300	2/86
333	WEST	1,290	1,300	2/86
334	WEST	1,300	1,300	11/85
335	WEST	1,300	1,300	8/85
336	WEST	1,290	1,300	3/86
201	NORTH	1,250 (1320)	1,250	
301	NORTH	1,195	1,250	8/83
TOTAL		17,865	18,100	

Figure in parentheses is the current asking rent for that vacant unit. Scheduled rent figure for the same unit indicates the appraiser's estimate of the current market rent for the unit.
No floor level effect on rent.

LIMITED OCEAN VIEW 2 BEDROOM

UNIT #	EXPOSURE	SCHED.RENT(ASKING)	ECON.RENT	RENT DATE
129	SOUTH	1,045	1,100	4/86
229	SOUTH	1,025	1,150	1/79
329	SOUTH	1,195	1,200	8/84
TOTAL		3,265	3,450	

$50 increase from 1st to 2nd floor. $50 increase from 2nd to 3rd floor.

NO OCEAN VIEW 2 BEDROOM

UNIT #	EXPOSURE	SCHED.RENT(ASKING)	ECON.RENT	RENT DATE
110	SOUTH	990	990	N/A
116	SOUTH	985	990	3/85
210	SOUTH	850	990	6/83
216	SOUTH	990	990	2/86
310	SOUTH	910	1,090	11/83
316	SOUTH	1,090	1,090	1/86
217	NORTH	950	990	6/85
317	NORTH	990	1,090	3/83
TOTAL		7,755	8,220	

No increase in rent from 1st to 2nd floor.
$100 increase from 2nd to 3rd floor.

Figure 3.5. Appraiser's rent roll for an oceanfront property

note. Actually, the appraisal is best supported by including *both* rent rolls as exhibits to the report.

While not a rent roll, Figure 3.4 shows the completed income section of the 71A appraisal form for our case study property. Note the commentary at the bottom of the page which explains lease terms, current asking rents, and so on. The actual rent roll would be attached to the report as an exhibit.

Finally, Figure 3.5 shows an appraiser's revised rent roll for an oceanfront building whose rents are largely dependent upon the view from each unit. While the owner's rent roll had units ordered according to unit number, the appraiser thoughtfully categorized units according to view. Not only did this make it much easier for the reviewer to understand the discrepancy between actual and market rents, but it served notice that the appraiser carefully considered each unit on an individual basis.

CHAPTER FOUR

COLLECTING RENT COMPARABLES

Market rent is popularly defined as "The rental income that a property would most probably command in the open market; indicated by current rents paid and asked for comparable space as of the date of the appraisal."[1] Market rent might be thought of as the rent the subject could potentially receive if it had just been rented at reasonable market levels. Your estimate of market rent shouldn't be so high that, if implemented, it would create vacancies unusually high for the neighborhood or greater than the vacancy factor you use in the appraisal.

It is impossible to properly evaluate a property's current actual income if we don't know how that income compares to the market level. Also, the appraisal should describe the competition and the neighborhood vacancy factor. This very valuable information is relatively easy to obtain by talking with the management of similar buildings in the area.

THE RENT SURVEY—WHICH BUILDINGS AND HOW MANY?

First, put yourself in the place of a prospective tenant looking for the type of apartment offered within the subject property. Major considerations will be price range and location. If there is an abundance of buildings that are reasonably similar, then make amenities, style, size, and age the next factors in the selection process.

You should gather enough comparables to provide a sound estimate as to the

[1] American Institute of Real Estate Appraisers (sponsor), *The Dictionary of Real Estate Appraisal,* American Institute of Real Estate Appraisers, Chicago, IL, 1984, p. 194.

proper market rent level for the subject property. The number of rent comparables depends on how similar to the subject they are, and how well they demonstrate support for your estimation of market rents.

The FNMA/FHLMC appraisal forms call for three rent comparables. Even for existing properties, many appraisal reports include two or three extra comparables—usually the minimum to provide acceptable support for a solid conclusion as to the subject property's market rent level.

Occasionally, there will be no properties which you consider adequately comparable. In this situation, bracket the subject with comparables considered inferior and comparables considered superior. This at least creates a range within which the subject should fit. Actually, such bracketing of comparables and subject should be done in every appraisal, no matter how many comparables are used.

INTERVIEWING TECHNIQUES

The on-site managers are usually the best source of information about the comparables. However, smaller buildings may not have on-site managers; tenants or owners are the source of information. For-rent signs are usually the only way to expeditiously contact the owners. Tenants are often the least desirable sources, as they usually don't know the rents that were negotiated in the most recent rental agreements.

Some appraisers prefer to approach the manager in the guise of a tenant. Most prefer to identify themselves as appraisers and divulge their true mission. I've almost always identified myself as an appraiser and have had cooperation over 90 percent of the time. The benefit of identifying yourself as an appraiser is that you can be more flexible in your interviewing. For instance, you can more easily ask what rents have *actually* been achieved, not just the *asking* price for a unit. Also, you can more reasonably ask for information as to which unit types are most in demand and how many vacancies currently exist. The manager may be inclined to provide more objective answers as well.

Occasionally, in a critical situation or when I feel the manager has not given me the true facts during my own interview, I'll send an associate to approach the property as a prospective tenant. I also use this double-interview technique for proposed properties where I'm at the disadvantage of not having actual rental figures to assist in the estimation of market rent, thereby providing a second opinion. Another method for determining the validity of the rent roll is to have an associate telephone the manager or owner and pose as an apartment shopper. The quoted rents should fit logically with those provided on the rent roll. One owner facing foreclosure through bankruptcy proceedings provided me with a rent roll stating that the lowest priced two-bedroom apartment was $1,025 per month. He was seeking the court's postponement of the foreclosure and desired as high a value as possible. I was working for the lender. Three members of my staff, posing as tenants, made separate calls to the manager and each was quoted $800 for an upcoming two-bedroom vacancy. Each person made written documentation of the call. In court, the lender's attorney interrogated and "set up" the owner before uncorking my testimony regarding the discrepancy. A very simple bit of investigative work provided a still-cherished moment for me.

As I'm asking for confidential information which is forthcoming only at the discretion of the manager, I try to put him or her at ease by always fully identifying myself and stating that I am appraising a similar property in the neighborhood. I start by asking the rents, then the unit sizes, and then the amenities. Finally, I inquire as to the number of vacancies at the property. Be sure to find out what rents have actually been achieved at the property. Unachieved asking rents should be used only to indicate the upper end of the range.

UNIT SIZE

While the FNMA/FHLMC appraisal forms ask for the square footages of the comparables' units, managers generally either do not know the size or give very rough and/or highly-inflated estimates. For instance, managers at many Los Angeles garden apartment complexes often state that their large one-bedroom units contain from 1000 to 1200 square feet, when in fact they are no more than 750 square feet. (There appears to be little reason why these particular managers seem to be the worst afflicted.) The rent roll in Figure 3.2 is unusual in that the owner included square footage figures. After measuring the units, I was very surprised that the owner's figures were within three percent of my own.

Obviously, it is seldom practical to enter occupied units to measure for size, and we'd soon be unwelcome if all of us constantly requested this favor. You might approach this situation as follows:

1. First, ask the managers whether they would consider the unit size to be small, medium, or large. Managers may want to fudge a little bit here, but answers generally won't be exaggerated as much as they might be for the actual square footage figures.
2. Next, ask how many square feet are in the unit. Still another caveat: The manager's figures may be generated by measuring techniques inconsistent with your measurements of the subject's units (such as whether perimeter walls, hallways, balconies, or patios are included).
3. Pace off the square footage from the building's exterior. By observing the location of the windows and doors, it may be fairly easy to determine approximately the location of the dividing walls.

CHECKLIST FOR REQUIRED INFORMATION

The following information checklist is quite comprehensive. Some items are obvious upon your setting foot on the property and needn't be asked. Depending on the property, the person, and whether you're interviewing in person or over the phone, the exact interview process changes to suit the situation.

UNIT SIZES AND RENTS

1. Unit types (number of bedrooms) including number of baths
2. Unit sizes
3. Furnished or unfurnished units?
4. Any extra rooms (such as service porch or dining room)?
5. Rent level actually achieved
6. Reasons for any ranges in the rent received for a particular type of unit (often due to differences in size or view)
7. Any rent concessions included (e.g., one month free rent on a six-month lease)
8. Term of rental (one month, six months, etc.)
9. Extra rent for pets or additional tenants
10. Which types of units are in greatest demand
11. Rental charges for parking or storage spaces

KITCHEN EQUIPMENT

1. Stoves—none, free-standing, or built-in
2. Refrigerators
3. Dishwashers
4. Microwaves
5. Trash compactors

HEATING AND COOLING

1. Type of heat
2. Air conditioning

UNIT AMENITIES

1. Balcony or patio, approximate size
2. Cable TV wiring

3. Fireplaces, wet bar, or vaulted ceilings
4. View or other orientation
5. Other

COMMON AREA AMENITIES

1. Laundry room
2. Pool
3. Spa
4. Barbecues
5. Play area
6. Gym
7. Recreation room
8. Saunas
9. Tennis court
10. Elevator

PARKING

1. Type—open, carport, garage
2. Security gate
3. Number of spaces included with the various unit types
4. Charge for extra parking (especially if subject offers this)
5. Single or tandem spaces (tandem spaces consist of one directly behind the other, necessitating moving one car in order to use the car in front of it)

GENERAL BUILDING INFORMATION

1. Effective age
2. Architectural style
3. Security
4. Quality
5. Condition
6. Overall appeal
7. Number of units
8. Number of current vacancies—in what unit types (For our purposes, a vacant unit is one which is vacant *and available* for rent; units which have recently been rented but which the tenants have not yet moved into should not be counted as vacancies)

COMPARABLE RENTAL DATA

Comparables selected are the most recent rentals, similar and proximate, known to the undersigned, that a tenant of subject property would have given consideration to renting.

ITEM	COMPARABLE No. 1	COMPARABLE No. 2	COMPARABLE No. 3
Address	1052 Franklin Avenue Metropolis	948 Franklin Avenue Metropolis	1112 Hightower Boulevard Metropolis
Proximity to subj.	3 blocks west	2 blocks west	4 blocks north
Map Code	78-F4	78-F4	78-E5
Date of rental survey	10-29-88	10-29-88	10-29-88
Brief description of property improvements	No. Units 54 No. Vac. 2 Yr. Blt. 69 3-story stucco over sub. garage. Pool. Full security. Centercourt.	No. Units 78 No. Vac. 2 Yr. Blt. 72 3-story stucco over sub. garage. Pool. Full security. Centercourt.	No. Units 35 No. Vac. 3 Yr. Blt. 70 4-story stucco over sub. garage. Pool. Full security. Centercourt.
Quality & condition	Quality Average Condition Average-	Quality Average Condition Average+	Quality Average Condition Average+

Individual unit breakdown

	Comp. 1 Tot.	BR	b	Sq. Ft.	Monthly Rent $	per sq. ft.	Comp. 2 Tot.	BR	b	Sq. Ft.	Monthly Rent $	per sq. ft.	Comp. 3 Tot.	BR	b	Sq. Ft.	Monthly Rent $	per sq. ft.
	3	1	1	650	660	102 ¢	3	1	1	684	685	100 ¢	3	1	1	650	690	106 ¢
	4	2	2	850	755	89 ¢	4	2	2	842	790	94 ¢	3	1	1	650	700	108 ¢
						¢						¢	4	2	2	850	800	94 ¢
	Includes one parking space.					¢	Includes one parking space					¢	4	2	2	850	810	95 ¢
	Additional parking @ $20/					¢	with 1 BR, 2 spaces for					¢						¢
	space.					¢	2 BR.					¢	$700 1 BR and $810 2 BR					¢
						¢						¢	are corner units.					¢

ITEM	COMPARABLE No. 1	COMPARABLE No. 2	COMPARABLE No. 3
Utilities, furniture and amenities included in rent	C & H water. Unfurnished. Small balcony. Built-in range. No DW.	C & H water. Unfurnished. Small balcony. Built-in range, DW.	C & H water. Unfurnished. Large balcony. Built-in range, DW. 1 pkg. space for 1BR, 2 spaces for 2BR.
Comparison to subject	Location: Similar	Similar	Similar
	Quality: Similar	Similar	Similar
	Condition: Inferior	Similar	Similar
	Amenities: Similar	Similar	Similar
	Ten. Appeal: Inferior	Similar	Superior
	Less appealing design and landscape.		

General comments (including any rental concessions) if applicable: No rent concessions. Comps ordered from least to most expensive. Subject is most similar to No. 2. All rents on a month-to-month basis. All comps have tenancies and management similar to the subject. Comps show a 4.2% vacancy rate.

MONTHLY RENT SCHEDULE — SUBJECT PROPERTY

Rental schedule is shown by type of units. Scheduled rents are actual rentals for an existing property, or projected rents for a proposed or incomplete building. Economic rents are forecasted rents to indicate the fair market rental the subject units would command if available for rent on the open market.

No. of Units	Unit Rm. Count Tot.	BR	b	Total Rooms	Sq. Ft. Area Per Unit	No. Units Vacant	Scheduled Rents Per Unit Unfurn.	Furn.	Total Rents	Economic Rents Per Unit Unfurn.	Furn.	Total Rents	Per Sq. Ft.	or Room
11	3	1	1	33	670	0	$ 660-680	$	$ 7,455	$ 685	$	$ 7,535	102 ¢	$ 228
11	3	1	1	33	695	0	650-670		7,360	675		7,425	97	225
14	4	2	2	56	865	0	755-800		11,060	800		11,200	92	200
14	4	2	2	56	890	0	750-790		10,950	790		11,060	89	198
	See below for explanation of price ranges.													
50	◄ TOTAL ►			178		0			$36,825			$ 37,220		

OTHER MONTHLY INCOME

	Scheduled	Economic
Parking	$ 0	$ 0
Laundry Income @ $4.00/unit/month	$ 200	$ 200
Commercial Space	$	$
	$	$
	$	$
Total Gross Monthly Income	$ 37,025	$ 37,420
Total Gross Annual Income	$ 444,300	$ 449,040

Utilities included in scheduled (actual) rents: [X] Water [ ] Gas [ ] Heat [ ] Electric [ ] Air Conditioning [X] Hot water

Utilities included in economic rents: [X] Water [ ] Gas [ ] Heat [ ] Electric [ ] Air Conditioning [X] Hot water

If proposed project or project under construction, the rent up time necessary, after completion, to lease 80% of the units at the projected economic rents is estimated to be N/A months.

Comments (including any rental concessions in scheduled rents, or anticipated in economic rents; if none, so state). See Addendum for current rent roll. Scheduled rents verified with resident manager. No rent concessions for subject. All tenants are on month-to-month agreements. Actual and economic rents reflect one parking space per 1BR, two spaces per 2BR. Current asking rents are $680 for 670SF 1BR units facing centercourt, $670 for 695SF 1BR facing outside, $800 for 865 2BR units facing centercourt, $790 for 890SF units facing outside. Based on rent survey discussion with resident manager, asking rents appear to be at economic level. Scheduled rents are 1.1% below estimated economic level. No personal property included in rents.

Figure 4.1. Page 5, 71A Form

9. Typical number of vacancies—in which unit types
10. Forces resulting in cyclical demand (e.g., school, economic base dependent on one industry)

LISTING THE COMPARABLES IN THE WRITTEN APPRAISAL

Figure 4.1 shows how rents are arranged on page 5 of the case study's 71A appraisal form. There are several items of special note:

1. The parking arrangement for each comparable is clearly presented.
2. There is a range in rents for each of the two unit types of Comparable No. 3. The footnote directly below the rent figures explains that this range is caused by a unit's orientation within the building—the corner units command an additional $10 in monthly rental.
3. The general comments section notes the order of the comparables (from least to most expensive).

CHAPTER FIVE

INCOME ESTIMATION

ADJUSTING THE RENT COMPARABLES

After the comparable rental information (discussed in Chapter 4) is obtained, estimates of market rent are made for each of the subject property's living units. Considering all the differences between the subject and each comparable, the rents of the comparable property are adjusted to what they should be for the subject. This process begins with analyzing each comparable, then concludes with the estimate of market rents for the subject. You may note that the terms "economic" and "market" rents stand for the same thing.

The adjustment grid (Table 5.1), which is the type often used in narrative reports, will help in visualizing this process.

The figures in Table 5.1 cover the subject's basic unit. Additional adjustments may be made on a unit-per-unit basis. These might include adjustments for view, location in the building, balconies, stoves, refrigerators, furniture, and so forth. Parking could be adjusted for here, or included later in the Miscellaneous Income category. The completed adjustment grid is often provided in narrative reports. Form reports are usually of less scope and do not include such a grid. In any case, it is wise to utilize such a grid and keep it in the file.

Theoretically, adjustments to the rent comparables are obtained from the comparables themselves. For instance, assume the subject provides two parking spaces for each unit and Comparable No. 1 provides only one parking space. All else being equal, the additional parking will allow the subject to rent for more. The question is how much more. If one of the comparables provides one parking space with each of its units and rents an additional space for $20 per month, this leads the appraiser to make a $20 upward adjustment to Comparable No. 1.

Table 5.1. Two-Bedroom Rent Comparable Adjustments

Item	Subject	Comparable 1 1052 Franklin	Comparable 2 948 Franklin	Comparable 3 1112 Hightower
Current Rent	—	$755	$790	$800
Balcony size	Small —	Small —	Small —	Large – $10
Dishwasher	Yes —	No + $10	Yes —	Yes —
Condition	Average + —	Average – + $10	Average + —	Average + —
Parking	2 spaces —	1 space + $20	2 spaces —	2 spaces —
Appeal	Average + —	Average – + $10	Average + –	Good – $10
Net Adjustment		+ $50	0	– $20
Indicated rent		$805	$790	$780

The theory is sound, but it can be virtually impossible to arrive at such equations for determining adjustments for items like balcony size and property appeal. Still, an adjustment may be needed, and your good judgment may be your only source.

CONSIDERING SQUARE FOOTAGE DIFFERENCES

As noted in the last chapter, it's often impossible to obtain accurate square footage numbers for the rent comparables. This problem is not critical as long as you have an idea as to how the comparables compare in size to the subject. Tenants usually think in less precise terms and rarely inquire as to the square footage of the apartment. They are often more concerned with the floorplan. The importance placed on square footage rental figures is a spill-over effect from appraisers' involvement in commercial and industrial properties, where rents really are determined by the number of square feet.

In the same vein, don't be trapped into speaking developers' dialect and making general statements as to how a proposed project should rent for "$0.80 per square foot." In the very least, smaller units will generally rent for more per square foot than larger units in the same building, and the total rent will depend heavily on unit mix (e.g., one-bedrooms may be worth $0.80 per square foot per month while an adjacent two-bedroom can only fetch $0.70).

MISCELLANEOUS INCOME

This is a separate income category which includes any income not provided for in the rental income. Miscellaneous Income may include income from additional parking spaces and laundry room usage. If the client is a lender and interested in real property only, you may wish to omit any rental income from personal property (such as refrigerator or furnishings) or, if the income is included, deduct the depreciated value of the personal property from the final value estimate. Note that some of the items shown on the accountant's operating statement should be excluded. These include forfeited rents, deposits, and interest on deposits. Here especially, your methodology should reflect what other appraisers are doing, and should coincide with the income categories that are reported for the sale comparables.

WHICH INCOME TO USE—ACTUAL OR MARKET

FNMA/FHLMC appraisal forms call for the appraiser to use the economic rents (rather than actual rents), although this choice should be left to the discretion of the appraiser. Both market and actual income levels and the variation between them should be considered when processing the income estimate into a value estimate. For instance, a higher gross income multiplier is often appropriate if using below-market rents in your income estimate. Whether market or actual income is shown in the value calculations, the resulting value estimate should be the same.

In rent-controled areas I always use actual rents. If a building is proposed or vacant, the only income estimate is the market rent estimate. In narrative reports, I most often use the actual rents in the income and expense statement—especially if there isn't much difference between actual and market. Using actual rents has two factors in its favor:

1. Purchasers and brokers will see this figure and give consideration to it. They may not know the market rent level, or their estimate of it will probably be different from yours.
2. Actual income is usually used in analyzing a comparable sale.

Note that the form uses the term *economic rent* rather than *market rent*—the two are synonymous. Also, the final income estimate for both actual and market income is labeled in Figure 5.1 as "Total Gross Annual Income." The most recent appraisal terminology labels this figure as *Potential Gross Income* (PGI) or *Total Potential Gross Income*. This is the total income attributable to the apartment building at full occupancy. Figure 5.2 uses the case study figures for depicting one possible narrative report format for the appraiser's income and expense statement.

COMPARABLE RENTAL DATA

Comparables selected are the most recent rentals, similar and proximate, known to the undersigned, that a tenant of subject property would have given consideration to renting.

ITEM	COMPARABLE No. 1	COMPARABLE No. 2	COMPARABLE No. 3
Address	1052 Franklin Avenue Metropolis	948 Franklin Avenue Metropolis	1112 Hightower Boulevard Metropolis
Proximity to subj.	3 blocks west	2 blocks west	4 blocks north
Map Code	78-F4	78-F4	78-E5
Date of rental survey	10-29-88	10-29-88	10-29-88
Brief description of property improvements	No. Units 54 No. Vac. 2 Yr. Blt. 69 3-story stucco over sub. garage. Pool. Full security. Centercourt.	No. Units 78 No. Vac. 2 Yr. Blt. 72 3-story stucco over sub. garage. Pool. Full security. Centercourt.	No. Units 35 No. Vac. 3 Yr. Blt. 70 4-story stucco over sub. garage. Pool. Full security. Centercourt.
Quality & condition	Quality Average Condition Average-	Quality Average Condition Average+	Quality Average Condition Average+

Individual unit breakdown

	Unit Rm. Count Tot.	BR	b	Size Sq. Ft.	Monthly Rent $	per sq. ft.
Comparable No. 1	3	1	1	650	660	102 ¢
	4	2	2	850	755	89 ¢
	Includes one parking space. Additional parking @ $20/ space.					
Comparable No. 2	3	1	1	684	685	100 ¢
	4	2	2	842	790	94 ¢
	Includes one parking space with 1 BR, 2 spaces for 2 BR.					
Comparable No. 3	3	1	1	650	690	106 ¢
	3	1	1	650	700	108 ¢
	4	2	2	850	800	94 ¢
	4	2	2	850	810	95 ¢
	$700 1 BR and $810 2 BR are corner units.					

ITEM	COMPARABLE No. 1	COMPARABLE No. 2	COMPARABLE No. 3
Utilities, furniture and amenities included in rent	C & H water. Unfurnished. Small balcony. Built-in range. No DW.	C & H water. Unfurnished. Small balcony. Built-in range, DW.	C & H water. Unfurnished. Large balcony. Built-in range, DW. 1 pkg. space for 1BR, 2 spaces for 2BR.
Comparison to subject	Location: Similar Quality: Similar Condition: Inferior Amenities: Similar Ten. Appeal: Inferior Less appealing design and landscape.	Similar Similar Similar Similar Similar	Similar Similar Similar Similar Superior

General comments (including any rental concessions) if applicable: No rent concessions. Comps ordered from least to most expensive. Subject is most similar to No. 2. All rents on a month-to-month basis. All comps have tenancies and management similar to the subject. Comps show a 4.2% vacancy rate.

MONTHLY RENT SCHEDULE — SUBJECT PROPERTY

Rental schedule is shown by type of units. Scheduled rents are actual rentals for an existing property, or projected rents for a proposed or incomplete building. Economic rents are forecasted rents to indicate the fair market rental the subject units would command if available for rent on the open market.

No. of Units	Unit Rm. Count Tot.	BR	b	Total Rooms	Sq. Ft. Area Per Unit	No. Units Vacant	SCHEDULED RENTS Per Unit Unfurn.	Furn.	Total Rents	ECONOMIC RENTS Per Unit Unfurn.	Furn.	Total Rents	Per Sq. Ft.	or Room
11	3	1	1	33	670	0	$ 660-680	$	$ 7,455	$ 685	$	$ 7,535	102 ¢	$ 228
11	3	1	1	33	695	0	650-670		7,360	675		7,425	97	225
14	4	2	2	56	865	0	755-800		11,060	800		11,200	92	200
14	4	2	2	56	890	0	750-790		10,950	790		11,060	89	198
	See below for explanation of price ranges.													
50	◄ TOTAL ►			178		0			$36,825			$ 37,220		

OTHER MONTHLY INCOME	Scheduled	Economic
Parking	$ 0	$ 0
Laundry Income @ $4.00/unit/month	$ 200	$ 200
Commercial Space	$	$
	$	$
	$	$
Total Gross Monthly Income	$ 37,025	$ 37,420
Total Gross Annual Income	$ 444,300	$ 449,040

Utilities included in scheduled (actual) rents: [X] Water [ ] Gas [ ] Heat [ ] Electric [ ] Air Conditioning [X] Hot water

Utilities included in economic rents: [X] Water [ ] Gas [ ] Heat [ ] Electric [ ] Air Conditioning [X] Hot water

If proposed project or project under construction, the rent up time necessary, after completion, to lease 80% of the units at the projected economic rents is estimated to be N/A months.

Comments (including any rental concessions in scheduled rents, or anticipated in economic rents; if none, so state). See Addendum for current rent roll. Scheduled rents verified with resident manager. No rent concessions for subject. All tenants are on month-to-month agreements. Actual and economic rents reflect one parking space per 1BR, two spaces per 2BR. Current asking rents are $680 for 670SF 1BR units facing centercourt, $670 for 695SF 1BR facing outside, $800 for 865 2BR units facing centercourt, $790 for 890SF units facing outside. Based on rent survey discussion with resident manager, asking rents appear to be at economic level. Scheduled rents are 1.1% below estimated economic level. No personal property included in rents.

Figure 5.1. Page 5, 71A Form

Appraiser's Income & Expense Statement

RENTAL INCOME

Unit type	Number of units	Rentable sq. ft.	Actual monthly rent	Ave. $/SF	Annual amount
1 br / 1 ba	11	670	$660-680	$1.01	$ 7,455
1 br / 1 ba	11	695	$650-670	$0.96	7,360
2 br / 2 ba	14	865	$755-800	$0.91	11,060
2 br / 2 ba	14	890	$750-790	$0.88	10,950
Totals	50				$ 36,825

MISCELLANEOUS INCOME	
Laundry Machines @ $4.00 per unit per month	200
TOTAL MONTHLY POTENTIAL GROSS INCOME	$ 37,025
TOTAL ANNUAL POTENTIAL GROSS INCOME	$444,300
VACANCY and COLLECTION LOSS @ 4%	(17,772)
EFFECTIVE GROSS INCOME	$426,528

EXPENSES

Item	Comment	Amount
Real Estate Taxes	Est. value @ 1.089%	$ 35,556
Insurance	$0.28/gross sq. ft.	11,050
Business License	0.5% EGI	2,133
Professional Management	5.0% of EGI	21,326
Resident Manager	$1,375/month	16,500
Payroll Taxes & Wkmns.Comp.	$202.50/unit/year	2,430
Utilities	Total=$37.45/unit/month	
Gas	$15.40/unit/month	9,239
Electricity	$13.80/unit/month	8,278
Water and Sewer	$8.26/unit/month	4,955
Elevator	Full service contract	1,500
Rubbish Removal	$2.90/unit/month	1,740
Pest Control	$50/quarter	200
Landscape Mt.	$160/month	1,920
Painting and Decorating	Every 24 months	4,895
Cleaning	Every 24 months	1,530
Maintenance and Repairs	$0.20/SF or $158/u/y	7,917
Supplies	$15/unit/year	750
Telephone	$35/month	420
Legal & Audit	$14/unit/year	700
Pool Maintenance	$150/month	1,800
Reserves		
Carpets and Drapes	$175/unit/year	8,760
Dishwashers & Disposals	$87/unit/year	4,350
ANNUAL OPERATING EXPENSES	33.3% of Tot. Potential Gross $3.74/gross sq. ft. $2,959/unit/year	$147,949
ANNUAL NET OPERATING INCOME		$278,579

Figure 5.2. An income and expense statement from a narrative report

ALLOWANCE FOR VACANCY AND COLLECTION LOSS

This is a deduction from potential gross income to account for probable losses in income. Vacancy is a function of both the market (competitive apartment buildings) as well as the income level utilized in the report—a property appraised with below-market income would have less of a vacancy loss than a property appraised with rents near the top of the market. When doing rent surveys, bear in mind that the vacancies may be unusually high during the beginning and end of the month.

Estimating collection loss is one reason to quiz the manager about the frequency and cost of evictions. This usually represents a much smaller amount than does vacancy allowance. The combined amount is expressed as a percentage of the potential income and, after deducting the amount from potential gross income, the subsequent income figure is called *effective gross income* (EGI).

One final warning: Your occupancy survey may be skewed if it is based on calls on vacancy signs—you'll have omitted fully occupied properties.

There are infinite ways of acceptably presenting the income estimate in a narrative report. The method shown in Figure 5.2 is just one of them.

CHAPTER SIX

ANALYZING THE LOCAL APARTMENT MARKET

Understanding the subject's market is an obvious necessity for a reliable appraisal, and it is also extremely important for a loan underwriter or potential purchaser. A solid and conclusive discussion of the local apartment market should be provided in the appraisal.

There are actually two markets to consider—the rental market and the resale market. While the market analysis can be done only after the collection of the rent and sale comparables, the typical appraisal report is assembled with much of the local market information appearing before the sections containing the comparables and income estimation.

RENTAL MARKET

The rental market can be described as the base of tenants from which the subject market is likely to draw. The subject won't be considered by all tenants in the community—there are different needs and wants in regard to rent levels, apartment size and location, and a neighborhood's socio-economic composition.

RENTAL MARKET INFORMATION SOURCES

Rent comparables usually provide the best indications of the health of the rental market. Perhaps the most important information they offer is the neighborhood occupancy rate. The comparables' managers should also be questioned as to what type of units are in most demand, average length of tenancy, and recent or anticipated changes in the typical occupancy rate and in the direction in which the market is headed. The answers to these questions can be compared to those reported for the subject property, in order to help determine whether the subject is being operated at maximum efficiency.

Other good sources of tenant demographics are usually available from city hall or the United States Census Bureau, although this information may be inadequate and/or outdated. The following information may be available from city hall:

- Population figures, current and projected
- Current inventory of apartments
- Apartment buildings currently under construction or being demolished (Note that this may be a good lead for land sale comparables for use in the cost approach)
- Any city actions that might favor or discourage apartment development and/or ownership
- Changes in the employment and economic base

A demographic package is sometimes available. Also, the city may be a source of census information. Other information sources include the local newspaper, appraisers, brokers, investors, library, and so on.

RESALE MARKET

Comparable sales provide a good look at the strength of the resale market. However, they are historic pieces of information and the market is constantly changing, due to the following factors:

1. Change in the inventory of apartments due to new construction and demolition
2. Fluctuations of the local and national economies
3. Changing economic base
4. Fluctuations in the supply and demand of apartment rentals
5. Fluctuations in the supply and demand of apartment buildings for sale
6. Changes in tax laws
7. Interest rate fluctuations and their effects on availability of financing
8. Changes in local laws affecting apartment values and ownership (e.g., property tax rate changes, rent control, zoning changes, building moratoriums, etc.)
9. Changes in the neighborhood's socio-economic composition

10. Recent or anticipated changes in rent levels
11. Competition from alternative investments

Further, values may fluctuate at the end of the year as investors acquire and dispose of investments for purposes of proper tax planning.

DATA ANALYSIS

While there is no excuse for errors and misjudgments in the appraiser's description of the market, an exhaustive study is not within the scope of the typical appraisal assignment. Consequently, the efficient gathering of the right sorts of data from ready sources and the application of good judgment is essential, especially for properties that are proposed or under construction and have yet to prove their acceptability in the market. The following statistics will be helpful to both the appraiser and the reader of the report.

- Vacancy rates
- Types of units in most and least demand
- Total apartment inventory
- Projected change in inventory
- Current population
- Projected change in population
- Percentage of people renting
- The rate at which new units are being rented
- Local employment and economic trends

While there are various sources of vacancy rates (e.g., those tabulated by mail carriers and utility companies), the appraiser's own rent survey usually provides the most current, reliable, and meaningful data.

It is impractical for this book to present a standardized series of mathematical equations for data analysis, as each appraisal assignment results in different kinds and amounts of market information. After presenting your information, include a short summary of the market condition and indicate whether any significant changes are expected.

SUMMARIZING AND REPORTING

Figure 6.1 is the *Area Data* and *Neighborhood and Marketing Area* sections from the appraisal for our case study. These sections call for information which mostly

AREA DATA

The ☐ City ☐ County ☐ Area population is approximately ____________

Population: ☐ Increasing ____ % per year ☐ Stable ☐ Decreasing ____ % per year

Describe the economic base which contributes a major influence on the stability of real estate Large and varied economic base consisting primarily of commercial, manufacturing, and supporting services. Most reliance is on light manufacturing of a variety of goods. (1)

Discuss employment stability Stable due to size and variation of economic base. Local unemployment figure for first six months of this year averaged 3.9% compared to state-wide average of 4.4%.

Rent Control: ☐ Yes ☐ No Comment ____________

Are local Government Agencies discouraging apartment development? ☐ Yes ☐ No Comment ____________

General comments, if applicable ____________

NEIGHBORHOOD AND MARKETING AREA

Type: ☐ Urban ☐ Suburban ☐ Rural Property Values: ☐ Increasing ☐ Stable ☐ Declining

Present Land Use: Built up 99 % Single Family 70 % Condominiums ____ % Apartments 15 % Commercial 15 % Industrial ____ %

____________ ____ %

Change in Present Land Use: ☐ Not Likely ☐ Likely or ☒ Taking Place From Single Family to Apartments (2)

Comment, if applicable Slow transition. Only about 15% of neighborhood is zoned for apartments. Most properties are currently at highest and best use.

Describe overall property appeal and maintenance level ____________

Describe any incompatible land uses (if none, so state) ____________

Single Family: Price range $ ____ to $ ____ Predominant $ ____ Age ____ yrs. to ____ yrs. Predominant ____ yrs.

Apartments: Predominant range in immediate area (excluding extremes)

	WALK-UP		ELEVATOR	
Number of units in each building		Units		Units
Age		Years		Years
Height (number of stories)		Stories		Stories
Condition				

Rental Range by Unit Type:

Unit Types:		WALK-UP	ELEVATOR
		$	$
		$	$
		$	$
		$	$

Comment on any unusual aspects of the above ranges ____________

Est. neighborhood apartment vacancy rate 4 % ☐ Decreasing ☒ Stable ☐ Increasing. Rent Levels are ☒ Increasing ☐ Stable ☐ Decreasing.

Describe the unit type(s) by number of bedrooms and rental range that are in the greatest tenant demand Affordable two-bedroom/two-bath units suitable for families and roommate situations. (3)

Describe the unit type(s) by number of bedrooms and rental range that are in oversupply One- and two-bedroom luxury units (over $750 for 1BR, $850 for 2BR) are in oversupply (8% vacancy). Little or no apparent effect on the subject and older properties, which have lower rent levels. (4)

Describe the potential for additional units in area considering land availability, zoning, utilities, etc. Additional units can be constructed on tear-down sites only. Neighborhood has 2,463 apartment units of which 61 (2.5%) have been completed in past 12 months. 93 units under construction, and an additional 52 in plan check. Typical. New supply is in line with the projected population increase. (5)

Describe the unsatisfied demand for additional units in area by type and rental ____________

Is population of relevant market area of insufficient size, diversity and financial ability to support subject property and its amenities? ____ If yes, specify.

ITEM	DISTANCE FROM SUBJECT PROPERTY	ACCESS or CONVENIENCE: GOOD	AVG.	FAIR	POOR
Public Transportation					
Employment Centers					
Shopping Facilities					
Grammar Schools					
Freeway Access					

Describe any probable changes in the economic base of neighborhood which would either favorably or adversely affect apartment rentals (e.g. employment centers, zoning) ____________

General comments including either favorable or unfavorable elements not mentioned (e.g. public parks, view, noise, parking congestion) No unfavorable elements. Neighborhood is bounded by Richardson Street (north), Freeway 71 (east), S.R. River (south), Royval Road (west). Size is 3.4 square miles (6% of City). Neighborhood population is 7.5% of city. 1980 Census places mean household income of subject's neighborhood at 8th highest of city's 26 neighborhoods. Neighborhood households are mostly families. (6)

Figure 6.1. Area Data and Neighborhood and Marketing Area Section of Form 71A (p. 2).

affects tenancy. Information on the resale market can be discussed either here, in the Market Approach section, or in an attached addendum. This page has been left intentionally incomplete in order to emphasize the items that are shown. Note the following observations:

1. The economic base is varied and healthy. The unemployment figures provide a comparison of local and statewide statistics.
2. These remarks indicate that the market is healthy enough to support some new construction, but that a limited amount of land will probably prevent a great deal of new construction.
3. The neighborhood vacancy rate is provided, and the unit type in greatest demand is given.
4. While the neighborhood vacancy rate is four percent, there is an excessive supply of luxury-priced units. An opinion is given as to the effect on the subject property.
5. These figures indicate that the current rate increase in new apartment units approximates the expected population increase. While such information is often not available, the number of units being lost to demolition is also a beneficial figure for the report.
6. These remarks define the neighborhood boundaries and provide a household income comparison with the rest of the city.

These remarks provide hard data which indicate the health of the market as well as the competitiveness of the subject property. The types of statistical figures used in Figure 6.1 are often easy to obtain, and give a much better picture than if only unsupported opinions had been provided.

REPORTING OF PROBLEM SITUATIONS

Your research and analysis should uncover any problems such as declining population, current or anticipated oversupply of apartments, faltering economic base, decreasing rents, and so forth. Every significant problem should be discussed in the report in terms of its effect on the property's marketability and how it is reflected in your final estimate of value. After describing it, summarize the degree of its effect. At the minimum, state whether it has "no," "minor," "moderate," or "major" effect on the subject property. Also, explain any difference between the neighborhood vacancy rate and that rate which you apply to the subject property in your estimation of net income.

CHAPTER SEVEN

EXPENSE STATEMENTS

The appraiser's operating expense estimate is key to the second most important figure in the appraisal—net income. (The most important figure, of course, is the value estimate.) In addition to determining current contracted expenses, obtaining and reviewing historical expense statements is basic to a reliable estimate. They are practically always available to the appraiser, although getting them will sometimes require a second request.

For any existing property, ask for three years of the most recent operating history. This most often comes in the form of accountant-prepared statements (although tax statements will sometimes be submitted instead, especially if the owner is a partnership). Accountants' statements usually have more categories than owner-drawn statements and allow a better look at the operation. Partnerships often provide monthly statements; sole owners sometimes receive statements only once a year.

REVIEWING THE EXPENSE STATEMENT

Reviewing consists of the following process:

1. Determine the time interval of the expense statement. Expenses are analyzed and estimated on an annual basis, so anything other than a twelve-month period will need adjustment to that basis.
2. Get explanations of any expenses that are not understood or leave some question.

3. Delete any expenses that aren't attributable to the operation of the property. The most frequent examples are depreciation, loan interest, and renovation or other capital improvements. Then come security deposit refunds, partnership costs, outside law suits, and personal taxes.
4. Watch expenses which are paid annually or semi-annually—their payments are sometimes included on an adjacent year's statement. Conversely, adjacent years' expenses may be included on the statement you're reviewing. Frequent violators are real estate taxes and insurance. If needed, adjust the expense amounts to an annual basis.
5. It is to the owner's advantage to show high expenses for income tax purposes. Find and deduct any excess expenses. These are mostly found in payroll or excessive management fees. At least one investor with whom I'm familiar has his apartment landscape crew maintain his sizeable estate.
6. The statement usually isn't categorized in the fashion the appraiser would like. With pencil and paper, recategorize the appropriate expenses. Leave an adjacent column to the right for your own expenses estimate.

EXAMPLES OF EXPENSE STATEMENTS

Figure 7.1 is a poorly-drawn expense statement actually submitted by an owner. At the top it indicates that the expenses are the actual figures. However, the excessively rounded figures indicate that they are estimates and should be used with caution. Also note that no date or time period is provided: Are the figures for a whole twelve months or only a portion of a year? How old are these figures? A statement like

INCOME AND EXPENSE STATEMENT

________ ACTUAL

________ PRO-FORMA

ITEM	CURRENT YEAR	PRO-FORMA
Income		
Gross Annual Rents	311,244	
Other		
Less: Vacancy	(0)	
TOTAL ANNUAL INCOME	311,244	

Figure 7.1. Poorly prepared owner's expense statement

Expenses		
Taxes	24,000	
Insurance	5,000	
Maintenance	9,000	
Utilities - Water & Sewer	25,000	
Fuel-Gas & Electricity		
Gardener		
Management - on site		
Management - off site	4,800	
Administration		
Office and Supplies		
Pool Service		
Elevator Services		
Cleaning Service		
Advertising		
Telephone		
Local-Accounting-License	100	
Pest Control Service	3,000	
TOTAL ANNUAL OPERATING EXPENSE	70,900	
Replacement Costs (Reserves)		
Appliances		
Carpeting		
Drapes	15,000	
Air Conditioning & Heating		
Furniture		
Roof		
TOTAL ANNUAL REPLACEMENT COSTS	15,000	
TOTAL ANNUAL EXPENSES		
Tenant Reimbursements		
NEW OPERATING INCOME	225,344	

I certify that the above information contained herein is true and correct.

Telephone ______________________________

Property Address ______________________________

____

Figure 7.1. *(continued)*

this necessitates a call to the owner or manager to at least find out the source of the estimate. My two favorable observations are (1) that it is well categorized and (2) that a telephone number and the property address are provided. (This information has been omitted here in order to protect the confidentiality of the document.)

Figures 7.2 and 7.3 show much better statements. In Figure 7.2 note that dates and sources are given. The unrounded numbers give the impression of accuracy. Upon further inspection you can see that many of the projections for 1986 are less than the actual figures from 1985. The owner should be questioned as to the rationale for these reductions. A program of capital improvements in 1985 could result in some of that year's figures being higher than normal. However, that doesn't explain the drop in gas expense. Also, if furniture income is deleted from the gross income estimate for this property, the furniture replacement expense should likewise be omitted. In any case, all the necessary figures appear to be present and are well categorized, resulting in a good expense statement with which to work.

Occasionally, interest expense is shown. As interest income is not a real operating expense, this figure must be deleted and the final total revised accordingly. Similarly, interest income is not a legitimate income for our purposes and it must be deleted as well. Always initial your changes, so that the reader of the report will know whether the changes were made by the appraiser or by someone else.

REDRAWING THE EXPENSE STATEMENT

While the appraiser's estimate of expenses is a discussion left to the next chapter, the two right-hand columns of the 71A form in Figure 7.4 show how the expenses appear in the finished appraisal of our case study. Note how the explanation column is designed to provide an explanation or salient equation. At the bottom is a blank area inviting additional discussion of any items. Figure 7.5 shows the information as it might appear in a narrative report.

SALIENT INDICATORS

Note how both Figures 7.4 and 7.5 provide the following data, which are based on the appraiser's expense estimate of $147,949.

1. The percentage of total expenses to total potential gross income (33.3 percent)
2. Expense per unit per year ($2,959)
3. Expenses per gross square foot per year ($3.74)

October 13, 1986

INCOME and EXPENSE STATEMENT – 2700 San Marino Street

	1985 Actual		1986 Projected	
INCOME				
Scheduled	184,811		196,200	
Vacancies	2,739	182,072	2,500	193,700
Laundry		1,300		1,300
TOTAL INCOME		183,372		195,000
EXPENSES				
Property Related:				
Taxes		5,235		9,800
Insurance		6,817		5,200
Licenses		343		336
Sub Total		12,395		15,336
Utilities:				
Water		3,943		4,000
Gas		9,059		7,800
Electricity		10,420		12,100
Sub Total		23,422		23,900
Maintenance:				
Plumbing		5,236		4,700
Painting		2,891		1,800
Carpets		2,577		600
Drapes		2,830		1,400

Figure 7.2. Well-prepared owner's expense statement

	1985 Actual	1986 Projected
Maintenance:		
Flooring	398	300
Cleaning	491	1,700
Electric	2,135	850
Hardware	3,829	3,400
Plastering	401	600
Ceramic Tile	2,553	1,000
Services	5,628	5,100
Exterior Work	1,585	-0-
Appliance Repair	95	-0-
Sub Total	30,649	21,450
Furnishings:		
Appliances	2,911	2,500
Furniture	7,373	4,500
Sub Total	10,284	7,000
Management:		
Resident Manager	11,271	14,500
Miscellaneous	870	800
Sub Total	12,087	15,300
TOTAL EXPENSES	88,837	82,986
Available for loans and ROI	94,535	112,014

1985 figures are from Federal Tax Return 1040E
1986 figures are 9 month actuals and projections for the last quarter of the year.

Figure 7.2. (continued)

FEDERAL PARTNERSHIP STATEMENTS - YEAR ENDING 12/31/84

STATEMENT 1 - INCOME FROM RENTS

Property 001		
INCOME		
GROSS RENTS	962,025	
LAUNDRY FACILITIES COMM	4,875	
INTEREST INCOME		
TOTAL INCOME		966,900
DEPRECIATION (SEE STMT BELOW)		
REPAIRS		
GENERAL	13,728	
APPLIANCES	429	
PAINTING	300	
PLUMBING	3,278	
ROOFING	50	
MISCELLANEOUS	2,789	
REPAIRS-ELEVATORS	2,161	
REPAIRS-CARPET & DRAPERIES	12,565	
CLEANING APTS	3,894	
REPLACEMENT	15,264	
TOTAL REPAIRS		54,458
OTHER EXPENSES		
ADVERTISING	1,261	
CLEANING & HAULING	3,769	
GARDENING	4,335	
INSURANCE	264,932	
LEGAL & ACCOUNTING	5,934	
LICENSES	743	
OFFICE EXPENSE	1,015	
SALARIES	16,655	
SUPPLIES	9,640	
TAXES-PROPERTY	38,460	
TAXES-PAYROLL	3,297	
TELEPHONE	1,063	
UTILITIES	24,418	
FURNITURE RENTALS	7,290	
GEN'L MGR FEES	38,149	
TOTAL EXPENSES		$226,251
NET INCOME		$740,649

Figure 7.3. Well-prepared expense statement from a partnership

ANNUAL EXPENSE ANALYSIS

ITEM	[X] ACTUAL 19 87 / [ ] PROPOSED	APPRAISER'S FORECAST	APPRAISER'S CALCULATIONS OR COMMENTS
FIXED EXPENSES:			
1. Real Estate Taxes	$	$ 35,556	[ ] Actual [X] Est. Total Assessed Value $ 3,265,000; 100 % of Value Tax Rate Per $100 $ 1.089
2. Other taxes or assessments		–	
3. Insurance	11,050	11,050	$0.28/GSF See below
4. Licenses		2,133	City license @ 0.5% EGI
5. Unsubordinated ground rent		–	Fee ground
OPERATIONAL EXPENSES:			
6. Fuel	$	$ –	
7. Gas	8,884	9,239	'87 + 4% $15.40/unit/month
8. Electricity	7,960	8,278	'87 + 4% $13.80/unit/month
9. Water & sewer	4,764	4,955	'87 + 4% $ 8.26/unit/month
10. Trash removal	1,740	1,740	Current contract $ 2.90/unit/month
11. Pest control	200	200	Current contract $50/qtrly./month
12. Building maintenance & repairs	16,581	7,917	$0.20/GSF See below
13. Interior & exterior decorating		4,895	See below
14. Cleaning expenses		1,530	See below
15. Supplies	697	750	$15/unit/year
16. Elevator maintenance	1,370	1,500	Current full service maint. contract
17. Pool maintenance	1,720	1,800	Current contract
18. Parking area maint. & snow removal		–	
19. Gardening	1,920	1,920	Current contract @ $160/month
20. Nonresident management	19,340	21,326	5% of E.G.I.
21. Resident manager's salary (No. 1)	8,160	8,400	$700/month
22. Resident manager's apt. allowance	7,920	8,100	1BR @ $675/month
23. Custodian's salary (No. ____)		–	
24. Custodian's apt. allowance		–	
25. Engineer's salary (No. ____)		–	
26. Elevator operator's salary (No. ____)		–	
27. Telephone operator's salary (No. ____)		–	
28. Security personnel's salary (No. ____)		–	
29. Other salaries (No. ____)		–	
30. Payroll taxes		605	7.2% of #21
31. Advertising			Good street exposure
32. Telephone	588	420	$35/month
33. Legal & audit	681	700	$14/unit
34. Leased furniture		–	
35. Workman's Comp. Ins.	1,703	1,825	$0.1106 x (#21 + #22)
36.		–	
REPLACEMENT RESERVES:			
37. Carpeting & drapes	$	$ 8,760	1BR @ $150/y 2BR @ $195/y
38. Ranges & refrigerators		–	
39. Dishwashers & disposals		4,350	50 DW @ $61 50 Disp. @ $26
40. Individual heating & AC units		–	
41.		–	
42.		–	
TOTAL EXPENSES & REPLACEMENT RESERVES	$	$ 147,949	$2,959/unit $3.74/GSF

Comments (identify items by number): Property has 39,585 gross square feet (GSF).
3)Based on $55/GSF replacement cost, Composite rate is $0.51/$100 coverage. This is reasonable.
#12)'87 figure contains cleaning painting and some capital improvements
#13)Interior painting @ $165 per 1BR, $220 per 2BR, 50% annual turn-over.
#14)Cleaning @ $50 per 1BR, $70 per 2BR, 50% annual turn-over.

INCOME APPROACH

Total Gross Annual ~~Economic~~ Scheduled Income (See Rent Schedule)	$ 444,300
Less Forecasted Vacancy and Collection Loss (4.0 %)	$(17,772)
Effective Gross Annual Income	$ 426,528
Less Forecasted Annual Expenses and Replacement Reserves (33.3 % of Total Gross Annual Economic Income)	$(147,949)
Net Annual Income from Total Property	$ 278,579
Less Return on and Recapture of Depreciated Value of Furnishings ($ ____ @ ____ %)	$(–)
Net Annual Income from Real Property	$ 278,579

Detail clearly method and mathematics of capitalizing Net Annual Income from Real Property
Market derived capitalization rate is 8.50%.

NOI	÷	OAR	=	Value
$278,579		.085	=	$3,277,400

INDICATED VALUE BY INCOME APPROACH $ 3,277,400
Rounded to $ 3,275,000

Figure 7.4. Page 7, 71A Form

Appraiser's Income & Expense Statement

RENTAL INCOME

Unit type	Number of units	Rentable sq. ft.	Actual monthly rent	Ave. $/SF	Annual amount
1 br / 1 ba	11	670	$660-680	$1.01	$ 7,455
1 br / 1 ba	11	695	$650-670	$0.96	7,360
2 br / 2 ba	14	865	$755-800	$0.91	11,060
2 br / 2 ba	14	890	$750-790	$0.88	10,950
Totals	50				$ 36,825

MISCELLANEOUS INCOME	
Laundry Machines @ $4.00 per unit per month	200
TOTAL MONTHLY POTENTIAL GROSS INCOME	$ 37,025
TOTAL ANNUAL POTENTIAL GROSS INCOME	$444,300
VACANCY and COLLECTION LOSS @ 4%	(17,772)
EFFECTIVE GROSS INCOME	$426,528

EXPENSES

Item	Comment	Amount
Real Estate Taxes	Est. value @ 1.089%	$ 35,556
Insurance	$0.28/gross sq. ft.	11,050
Business License	0.5% EGI	2,133
Professional Management	5.0% of EGI	21,326
Resident Manager	$1,375/month	16,500
Payroll Taxes & Wkmns.Comp.	$202.50/unit/year	2,430
Utilities	Total=$37.45/unit/month	
Gas	$15.40/unit/month	9,239
Electricity	$13.80/unit/month	8,278
Water and Sewer	$8.26/unit/month	4,955
Elevator	Full service contract	1,500
Rubbish Removal	$2.90/unit/month	1,740
Pest Control	$50/quarter	200
Landscape Mt.	$160/month	1,920
Painting and Decorating	Every 24 months	4,895
Cleaning	Every 24 months	1,530
Maintenance and Repairs	$0.20/SF or $158/u/y	7,917
Supplies	$15/unit/year	750
Telephone	$35/month	420
Legal & Audit	$14/unit/year	700
Pool Maintenance	$150/month	1,800
Reserves		
Carpets and Drapes	$175/unit/year	8,760
Dishwashers & Disposals	$87/unit/year	4,350
ANNUAL OPERATING EXPENSES	33.3% of Tot. Potential Gross $3.74/gross sq. ft. $2,959/unit/year	$147,949
ANNUAL NET OPERATING INCOME		$278,579

Figure 7.5. A narrative report's Income and Expense Statement

These data are meaningful to the experienced appraiser and greatly assist the reviewer. If you're a beginning apartment appraiser, pay attention to this information and you will start to see patterns develop. Here are a few such relationships:

1. The percentage of total expenses to income will diminish as rent levels increase.
2. Expenses per unit will diminish as the units become smaller.
3. Expenses per square foot will diminish as unit sizes become larger (although this could be overridden by family tenancies).

The items mentioned above are specific to those categories. Items which will reduce all three are newer age, fewer amenities, and separate metering of tenants for more of their utilities. The condition of the property is also an important factor. The appraiser's estimation of maintenance expenses will depend on the management style that the appraiser feels is most appropriate. Some neglected properties either require or deserve substantial ongoing expenditures while others aren't economical to resurrect and are worth only a minimal maintenance investment. Most properties which have been kept in excellent condition are worth keeping in excellent condition. Once again, the appraiser's analysis of the property's management becomes a consideration.

CHAPTER EIGHT

OPERATING EXPENSE ESTIMATION

Operating expenses are deducted from gross income in order to calculate the net income estimate for the property. If you rely wholly on the gross income multiplier of value-per-unit methods for your value estimate, you will not need an estimate of operating expenses in arriving at a value estimate. However, operating expenses play a vital role for any lender who is using your appraisal to determine a maximum loan amount for the property; a reasonable expense estimate may be crucial.

INFORMATION SOURCES

The primary source of information is the actual expense history for the property itself—especially for difficult-to-estimate expenses such as utilities, trash removal, and landscape maintenance. If the three-year expense history isn't available (usually due to the property being either a recent acquisition or newly constructed), get as much information as is available, including current figures for property taxes, insurance, management, utilities, and maintenance contracts. When using actual expenses, bear in mind that your estimate should reflect the level under prudent and typical management. Categories you might want to change usually center around management and salaries, areas in which tax considerations and favoritism can skew the historical figures from what they should be. Other items include maintenance, supplies, telephone, replacements, and so on.

Appraisal theorists have frequently suggested that expense histories for comparable properties be researched and appropriately applied to the subject. While simply stated, such data are often almost impossible to obtain, and sufficient information usually isn't available as to what they really reflect. Your time may be more wisely spent in calling property management firms and inquiring as to their estimates for the subject property.

The Institute of Real Estate Management (430 N. Michigan Avenue, Chicago, IL 60611–4090) annually publishes *Income/Expense Analysis, Apartments,* which is based on information submitted by the Institute's members. Information is presented according to metropolitan area as well as type and size of building. Expense figures are given on both a cost-per-unit basis and a percentage of gross income. This breakdown may not be appropriate for items such as landscape maintenance.

My company (Apartment Building Appraisers and Analysts, Inc., P.O. Box 26, Los Angeles, CA 90078) annually publishes *Apartment Building Operating Expense Guideline,* the figures of which apply only to properties in southern California. As well as having expense figures, the book provides various bits of general information and lists of influencing factors, many of which are reprinted in this chapter. We get our figures from reviewing operating statements of properties, including those we appraise, and from surveying vendors, suppliers, and maintenance contractors. The state Public Utilities Commission supplies figures for changes in utility costs. Life expectancy estimates are based on interviews with the managers of properties we appraise. These are the only two operating expense guides of which I am aware.

EXPENSES AS A PERCENTAGE OF GROSS INCOME

When making a rough estimate of expenses, people often estimate it as a percentage of gross income. While this is no substitute for an itemized estimation, it can work reasonably well if the person estimating has a good background in apartment appraisal, lending, and/or management. Before estimating expenses in each appraisal, I take a guess at what percentage of income they will be. I usually come within two percentage points. Try this contest with yourself. Keep at it, and you'll improve your own rough estimates.

For most property types, the percentage is taken on *effective* gross income (total income less the vacancy and collection loss factor). However, the FNMA forms ask for the percentage based on *total* income. Depending on the ratio of fixed expenses to variable expenses, the theoretically correct choice is somewhere in between. In any case, I feel consistency is the key; I always think in terms of total potential income (as is requested on the forms), at least when dealing with apartments. Also, when discussing percentages, always clarify if the figure includes or excludes the vacancy and collection loss factor.

EXPENSE CATEGORIES

There are six major categories of expenses:

1. Real estate taxes
2. Insurance
3. Utilities
4. Management
5. Maintenance
6. Reserves

Most of these categories can be broken down into multiple items. The following discussion identifies typical expense categories and gives factors to consider in their estimation.

Real Estate Taxes

Depending on local custom and procedure, taxes may or may not be reset upon the sale of the property. In any case, the real estate tax estimation should closely follow the same method which a knowledgeable buyer would use.

In California, voters passed Proposition 13 as a state constitutional amendment, thereby limiting *ad valorem* property taxes to one percent of a property's assessed value. However, benefit assessments—which pay for the cost of capital improvements that increase property values (e.g., streets, sidewalks, sewers, and lighting) or which finance certain services (e.g., maintenance and operation of flood control districts)—are not subject to this limitation. Invariably, the annual property tax bill is slightly above the one percent limit.

Insurance

Ideally, you'll be able to figure insurance expense based on actual policies for other properties. This figure is usually abstracted on a per-square-foot basis. Adjustments should be made to account for differences as addressed in the influencing factors listed below. A word of caution: Insurance rates can fluctuate wildly from year to year. Policies that you use to facilitate this comparative shopping should have been written recently enough to reflect current rates.

A second method is to use the same type of calculation the insurers themselves use. They quote policy prices based on a composite rate. The equation is:

$$\text{Replacement Cost} \times \text{Composite Rate} = \text{Policy Premium}$$

The composite rate is usually quoted as a certain amount per $100 of replacement cost. Replacement cost, which may exclude the value of the foundation and the underground plumbing, is determined by multiplying the square footage of the building by a replacement cost-per-square-foot figure. You'll have to check with local insurance experts as to composite rates and replacement cost figures.

The typical policy offered by insurance companies for apartment buildings usually includes extended coverage on buildings and contents at replacement cost for destruction by fire, wind, hail, smoke, vandalism, and aircraft, but excluding earthquake and flood. The package may also include coverage for loss of rents up to twelve months, general business liability, and other coverages. Some factors influencing the composite rate applied by insurers are as follows:

1. *Age.* Insurance expense is usually more for older buildings.
2. *Location.* Composite rates and premiums generally decrease as an area becomes more desirable.
3. *Condition.* Better condition usually means lower composite rates and premiums.
4. *Size.* Rates may increase with more units in the building.
5. *Conformance to Zoning Regulations.* If the improvements do not conform to local zoning density requirements, lenders may require two additional endorsements. The first, called a contingent liability endorsement, provides that if the building is more than 50 percent destroyed (or whatever the cutoff point is that the local municipality uses to determine whether the building must be rebuilt to code), the entire replacement cost of the building will be paid. This is so that the remaining structure can be razed and a new structure built according to the density requirements. Purchased along with this is a second endorsement, called a demolition cost endorsement, which pays for the cost of the demolition of the remaining structure.
6. *Hazards.* These include nearby brush areas and gas stations, as well as storage yards for bottled gas.
7. *Pool.* Some companies charge extra for pools, while others include them in the standard policy. They may require pools to be fenced, however.
8. *Recreational Facilities.* The possibility for liability suits may increase the cost of the premium when the improvements include these facilities (especially tennis, volleyball, and handball courts).
9. *On-site Manager.* Insurance underwriters prefer on-site managers.
10. *Property History.* Previous claims will tend to raise subsequent policy costs.

Utilities

When available, historical operating expense statements should be referenced for electricity, gas, and water and sewer expense as each of these expenses can cover a wide range. If appropriate, an inflationary adjustment should be made. Factors which influence the amount of the expense are as follows:

1. *Utilities Provided by Landlord.* Beware of master-metered buildings (those for which the landlord pays all expenses). These are among the most expensive to operate.
2. *Billing Rates and Structures.*
3. *Tenancy.* Expenses will increase as do the number of tenants per unit.
4. *Amenities Provided.* Amenities may include elevators, laundry rooms, recreation room, lighted tennis courts, pools, and spas. Most amenities tend to increase utility expense.
5. *Type of Building.* Buildings with enclosed hallways and older components will use more electricity. However, they may have less landscape maintenance expense.
6. *Plumbing Efficiency.* Leaks and meter inaccuracies are factors. Also, a central hot water system without a circulating pump tends to increase gas consumption, as does a high thermostat setting on the water heater. Low-flow shower heads will reduce expenses.
7. *Landscape Requirements.* Water consumption will vary according to the amount and type of landscaping, soil conditions, and sprinkler equipment.
8. *Energy Efficiencies.* Newer buildings typically have better insulation. Also, fluorescent lighting may cut electrical consumption by 50 percent or more over incandescent fixtures. Timers can help decrease both electric and gas consumption.

Management

On-Site Management

Properties of 20 or more units should have an on-site manager. California law requires that every apartment building of 16 or more units must have a person residing on the premises who is in charge of the property. Duties vary according to the involvement of off-site management, but may include:

1. Serving as liaison between tenants and off-site management
2. Reporting needed work to off-site management
3. Collecting rents
4. Showing and renting vacant units; preparing rental agreements
5. Directing maintenance and service workers
6. Caring for common areas

7. Contracting for minor repairs and maintenance
8. Providing bookkeeping

On-site managers with minimal responsibilities may receive reduced rent as their only form of compensation. Managers at larger complexes may receive a salary in addition to free rent. Compensation should approximate that which they could receive for similar jobs. However, I'm often amazed at how much work some managers do in return for very little compensation. Factors affecting the on-site manager's time and compensation requirements are as follows:

1. *Time Involvement.* Inclusion of additional duties will require more compensation.
2. *Tenancy.* Problem tenancies or other management-intensive tenancies will require more compensation.
3. *Income Levels.* On-site management fees will be lower in buildings catering to lower-income tenants.
4. *Property Size.* Per-unit compensation may decrease as the property becomes larger. Larger complexes will require at least one assistant manager.

Off-Site Management

Off-site management is conducted by either the property owner or a property management agent. Even if the property is owner-managed, the owner will expect some compensation for this involvement. Duties of the off-site management include:

1. Preparing management plan and annual budget
2. Hiring and directing on-site management and maintenance employees
3. Satisfying tenants' needs to a reasonable degree
4. Purchasing supplies, equipment, furnishings, licenses, services, and service contracts; purchases should be at the most beneficial prices
5. Preparing vacancies for rent, and minimizing vacancy time by renting units as quickly as possible
6. Designing and executing capital improvement programs
7. Supervising and enforcing evictions
8. Keeping the apartment operation in compliance with applicable rules and regulations
9. Providing accounting services and supplying ownership with operating reports
10. Otherwise operating the property as efficiently as possible.

In addition, in the case of smaller properties without resident managers, off-site management may show units, prepare rental agreements, and provide other day-to-day services.

Compensation is most often based on a percentage of the amount of income collected, although some companies charge a flat fee for each unit. Fees are heavily dependent on building size and management intensity; they may be higher for properties that do not have on-site managers. Factors affecting the fee of the off-site manager are:

1. *Tenancy.* Management intensity increases with evictions, problem tenants, and families. Also, tenants in high-rent buildings will expect prompt management action with regard to repairs and services.

2. *Turnover.* High turnover rates result in time expenditures for unit preparation, apartment showings, credit checks, and rental agreement preparations. Note that some or all of this work can be the responsibility of on-site management.

3. *Property Size.* Economies of scale result in lower fee structures for larger buildings.

4. *Building Condition.* Older buildings requiring more repairs or rehabilitation result in greater management intensity.

5. *Amenities.* Common area amenities such as pools, security, subterranean parking, elevators, and tennis courts will require more attention. The same holds true for larger buildings with more complex mechanical systems.

6. *Management Company.* Newer and smaller management companies will be more aggressive in lowering fees to attract business.

7. *Rental Rates.* Properties with low rent levels will pay a higher percentage of collected income to off-site management.

Maintenance

Interior Painting and Cleaning

Interiors of units are often cleaned and painted prior to new tenancies. The entire unit is not always repainted; frequently omitted are ceilings, closet interiors, window trim, and kitchen cabinet interiors and exteriors.

Determine whether any of this work is included in the manager's compensation or whether the previous tenant forfeits a deposit to cover this expense. The job is usually given to an independent cleaning contractor who has a standardized pricing structure. Influencing factors for this expense are:

1. *Turnover Rate.* A higher turnover rate results in a greater interior cleaning and painting expense.

2. *Tenancy Type.* Besides affecting turnover rate, tenancy type also affects the annual interior painting expense: Singles and families with children tend to be rougher on the surfaces of the units, resulting in the need for more expensive treatment (patching, plastering, double coats, etc.). There may be additional work if the tenants have pets.

3. *Unit Size and Building Characteristics.* Rooms of unusual size or shape, older buildings, wood window frames, and natural wood finish cabinets all involve added cost.

4. *Preparation Work Required.*

Landscape Maintenance

Landscape maintenance may be the responsibility of either the on-site management or a landscape maintenance contractor. Sometimes the duties will be split, with the manager being responsible for watering and cleaning the public areas. The gardener makes one or more visits per week at an hourly, daily, or monthly rate to mow lawns, edge borders, trim trees and shrubs, and care for flowers. Gardeners price their services according to the amount of time required, which depends on the following influencing factors:

1. *Amount of Landscaping.* This need not be associated with the size of the building. Some smaller buildings have more square feet of landscaping than do much larger buildings.

2. *Type of Landscaping.* Some types of plantings require less time and attention, and others require special treatment.

3. *Amount of Difficult Work.* Edging along the building and fences can require additional work and therefore time. Shrubs that require ladders in order to be trimmed result in more time and expense.

4. *Existing Landscape Improvements.* Plantings in improvements such as brick and wood planters may require more care than low-maintenance items, while the improvements themselves restrict movement and result in more time required. Built-in landscape sprinklers will help avoid the expense of manual watering, especially if the sprinklers are operated by timers.

5. *Rental Market.* Tenants in high-rent buildings tend to expect better landscape quality and maintenance.

Pool Maintenance

The average apartment pool measures about $15' \times 30'$ and has a capacity of about 25,000 gallons. This size pool is normally serviced once a week but could be serviced two or three times a week, depending on the amount of use. Frequent summer use may require additional service calls.

Service includes checking the chlorine balance, scrubbing the tile, vacuuming, and cleaning the filter. Chemicals and cleaning materials are often charged separate from the maintenance contract. The following factors dictate the amount of service required:

1. *Tenancy Type.* The amount of use a pool receives depends on the type of tenancy in the building. Pools in family buildings are used far more than pools in buildings with other tenancy types.
2. *Adequacy and Condition of Filtering Unit.* Pools with inadequate filters require more attention and greater cost.
3. *Landscaping.* Pools surrounded by large amounts of landscaping, especially trees and shrubs that shed their leaves, may require more visits per week in order to keep the pools free of debris.
4. *Season.* Seasonal differences in the amount of use result in seasonal differences in expense.

Trash Removal

A smaller building may get by with trash removal performed by the city. This can mean a lower rate than would be charged by a commercial hauling company. A typical one-bedroom unit with a single tenant will produce enough trash in one week to fill one 32-gallon can, so any more than six or seven units may make collection with cans cumbersome. Also, some cities bill the tenant directly as a part of the utility bill.

For larger buildings, trash collectors typically use bins that can be manipulated by hydraulic-lift disposal trucks. One of these bins typically services up to 15 units with one weekly pickup. Many municipalities aren't equipped to handle bins and the job must be contracted to a private firm. Factors influencing the cost of rubbish collection are:

1. *Tenancy of the Building.* Tenancy can be classified into singles, families, and seniors, and has an effect on both the number of bins and number of pickups. Buildings rented predominantly to families can easily produce two to three times the amount of trash of an all-singles building, resulting in the need for additional bins or pickups.
2. *Size and Design of the Building.* Since placement of bins is often for tenant convenience, a more compact complex may not require the same number of bins as a less densely-developed complex. The topography of the site, the amount of obstruction around the bin area, and the required amount of turn-around space all affect the accessibility of the bins and therefore the cost of the service.
3. *Distance to the Truck and Street.* Bins requiring manual movement by the truck operators will cost more to service.

4. *Custom Applications.* Containers specially designed for chute-type trash disposal are often more costly to service.

5. *Time of Pickup.* High-rent buildings often prefer service after a certain time of day (to avoid disrupting the tenants), resulting in possible greater cost due to traffic and routing problems.

6. *Distance to the Dump Site.* Buildings located far from the dump site may have to pay a greater fee for the service.

7. *Location.* Through a combination of the above factors, buildings located in more densely populated areas tend to be more expensive.

General Repairs and Maintenance

This is one of the most difficult categories to estimate. Consequently, I prefer to first estimate as many other maintenance expenses as possible, leaving as little as possible to be accounted for in this category. The items shown below are the major expenses in general repairs and maintenance:

- Magnesite repair
- Vinyl floor repair/replacement
- Stucco patching
- Security entry system repair
- Door lock replacement
- Asphalt resurfacing
- Fire extinguisher service
- Plumbing repairs
- Carpentry repairs
- Drain/sewer cleaning
- Roof repair
- Screen and window replacement
- Concrete patching
- Appliance repair
- Countertop resurfacing
- Sink replacement
- Electrical repairs
- Common area upkeep

Care should be taken so as not to include expenses that are covered in other categories (painting, cleaning, reserves, etc.). Also, capital improvements should not be included in the annual operating expense estimate. The following factors influence the amount of annual maintenance required:

1. *Age, Condition and Style of Building.*

2. *Building Size.* Smaller buildings and buildings with smaller units generally cost more per square foot.

3. *Tenancy.* Families and disrespectful tenants will cause more damage. Transient tenancies will tend to create more expense.

4. *Building Quality.* Better-quality buildings tend to have fewer maintenance requirements. However, maintenance items may be more expensive if rents are high and tenants more demanding.

Table 8.1. Typical Life Expectancies for Replacement Items

Item	Life (in years)
Carpets	6
Drapes	3
Disposers	3
Dishwashers	5
20- to 30-gallon water heaters	8
100-gallon water heaters	8
Wall air conditioner	7

5. *Amenities.* Saunas, barbecues, playgrounds, recreation rooms, and gyms will create additional expense. Pool and spa maintenance is covered in a separate category.

6. *Management.* On-site management may be utilized for some repairs and maintenance, thereby reducing the expense of outside contractors.

7. *Reserve Expense.* Maintenance expense should be less if substantial replacements are accounted for in the reserves for replacements.

General repairs and maintenance is often figured on a cents-per-square-foot-per-year basis. A dollars-per-unit figure is also appropriate, and may be somewhat more meaningful to the reader of your report.

Reserves

This category provides for the expense of periodically replacing short-lived items such as carpeting, drapes, roof covering, water heaters, and appliances. The annual expense is most often calculated by dividing the replacement cost (including installation expenses) of an item by its useful life. Table 8.1 gives typical life expectancies for replacement items.

There is substantial difference of opinion as to whether reserves should be included for newer buildings. I generally include only those reserve items which will probably be replaced in the first five to seven years (the typical holding period for the first investor). These items include carpets, drapes, and garbage disposal.

Technically, exterior paint and roofing should be included as reserve items. However, most investors with whom I work think of these two items more as capital improvements and do not take a reserve for either one. If I were to include them, my expense estimate wouldn't reflect what the investors in my local market are actually doing. Of course, the condition of the exterior paint and the roof must still be considered when arriving at the final value estimate.

PART TWO

CHAPTER NINE

SELECTION OF SALE COMPARABLES

One of the most frequently asked questions by new appraisers is how to find comparable sales. While it's an issue initially fraught with both apprehension and mystique, the process becomes much easier as the appraiser gains experience.

You should use as many comparables as are needed to adequately support your market approach value conclusion. "Adequately support" means that the reader of your appraisal report sees enough information to be able to form his or her own solid opinion as to value (which, hopefully, will coincide with yours). As such, the number of comparables depends on the quality and quantity of information. The FNMA forms provide space for three sale comparables, although many appraisers find it necessary to provide additional sales in concluding and supporting their opinion of value.

SELECTION PROCESS

There are seven elements of comparison that you have to consider in the selection process. Each comparable must be analyzed with respect to all seven:

1. *Date of the Sale*. The sale should not have occurred so long ago that market conditions have changed. Market changes can occur due to variations in supply/demand (both in number of tenants and apartment inventory), interest rates, local and national economic health, neighborhood evolution, and so on.
2. *Physical Characteristics*. Size (number of units) and age are the primary considerations here. Other factors are condition, unit mix, and building style and quality.

3. *Location.* The comparables should be located close enough to the subject that they are considered to be in the same geographic market. The size of this market generally increases as the building size becomes larger. Also, if there are substantial differences in municipal codes or overall desirability, you may wish to confine your comparable search to the same community in which the subject is located. While the comparables may be located in different neighborhoods, differences in appeal from one neighborhood to another are at least partially compensated for by the consequent differences in rent levels.

4. *Financing Terms.* The sale comparable's price was probably artificially high if favorable financing (such as below-market seller-carried financing) was involved. The sale price can be appropriately adjusted to its cash-equivalent value by using the techniques discussed in Chapter 13.

5. *Tenancy and Management Profiles.* Purchasers generally pay a premium for good tenancy and in-place management.

6. *Conditions of Sale.* A comparable's sale should be an arm's-length transaction, unaffected by duress or unusual relationships between the parties involved.

7. *Property Rights Conveyed.* Most apartment building sales reflect the conveyance of normal property rights, which do not unduly affect the use of the transaction as a comparable. The occasional violators include long-term leases at other than market rent as well as buildings on ground leases.

When selecting comparables for my own appraisals, I first look at date, physical characteristics and location: If the comparable is a recent transaction, is of similar size and age, and is located in reasonable proximity to the subject, chances are good that I will use it in the appraisal (assuming that there is a sufficient amount of verifiably accurate data).

INFORMATION SOURCES

Depending on the nature of his or her appraisal work, every appraiser develops a different system of techniques and contacts to generate sale comparables. While some sources are readily available to everyone, others require cultivation over time. Sources are generally limited to the following:

1. *Salespeople.* Salespeople often don't consider it an efficient use of their time to help appraisers. As a result, seeking information from them calls for a well-practiced approach. This approach includes identifying yourself as well as your reason for needing the information. A personal visit may be desirable—salespeople are usually more accommodating than when you telephone. In one case, being short of sales and knowing of one which would make all others pale in comparison, I drove 30 miles to the broker's office. I didn't want him to have the opportunity to refuse to talk with me over the phone. Although I was unannounced and didn't

know whether he would be there, he was; I walked out with copies of the escrow instructions, the rent roll, and the operating statements.

2. *Buyers and Sellers.* Contacts with buyers and sellers most often occur when verifying data after it has been obtained from another source. Perhaps the most useful information these people provide regards the financing behind the transaction. On the other hand, they often do not have ready access to income information.

3. *Appraisers.* Finding an appraiser who has recently appraised a similar property in the area can be the biggest stride in the completion of your assignment.

4. *Data Services.* These services are usually available only in large metropolitan areas. In southern California we have apartment sale information available through California Market Data Cooperative, Inc., and Comps, Incorporated.

5. *Lenders.* Financing for some of the comparable sales has probably been provided by an institutional lender who most probably required an appraisal. If so, all of the required information regarding the comparable may be available from the appraiser or loan department.

6. *Public Records.* The access and availability of useful information varies greatly from one municipality to the next. While researching deeds and mortgages can provide good leads, that research can be very laborious and rarely provides income information. In California, two private companies maintain computer records of all real property transactions occuring in the major counties. These companies have developed time-share systems which allow access to these files by appraisers and others using computer terminals. The downside is that they rarely provide sufficient information for expeditiously locating a principal or broker associated with the transaction. However, the lender is often specified.

7. *Advertisements.* Advertisements and brochures inform you of what properties are being marketed and who the active brokers are.

8. *Multiple Listing Services.* Depending on your locality and the nature of your assignments, this may be your best source. However, these services usually limit distribution to members, and becoming one requires a broker's license and a sizeable initiation fee.

REQUIRED INFORMATION

With few exceptions, you should obtain the following information about each sale comparable that you use in the appraisal:

GENERAL

1. Address
2. Number of units

3. Unit mix
4. Gross square feet
5. Description
6. Occupancy
7. Condition at time of sale
8. Age
9. Quality of tenancy and management
10. Photograph

SALE

11. Date escrow opened
12. Date escrow closed
13. Sale price
14. Document recording number

FINANCE

15. Amount of each mortgage
16. Payments
17. Interest rate
18. Term
19. Amortization
20. Details on any exchange
21. Downpayment
22. Details on non-market financing (especially important)

INCOME

23. Actual income from rentals, laundry, and other sources
24. Relationship of actual rents to market rents
25. Vacancy and collection loss factor, operating expenses, and net income

VERIFICATION

26. At least one party to the transaction in addition to . . .
    Deed
    Lender
    Title company or title report

INSPECTION OF COMPARABLES

Chapter 2 discusses property inspections; its lessons must also be considered when inspecting the comparables. It's a good idea to ask the manager what the current rental rates are—this provides an easy method of comparing the comparable's overall appeal to that of the subject. Also, as will be discussed shortly, these rates are helpful in selecting the gross income multiplier and overall rate.

Buyers will quite often do cosmetic work after purchasing the property. Determine the property's condition *at the time of transaction,* a condition which might have been different than what you'll see upon your inspection.

Most clients require a photograph of the comparable. Take it from a view that shows not only the front but the most revealing side as well. Some appraisers are content to park their car, take the photo, and drive off—never having set foot on the property. However, good appraisal practice calls for observations that are possible only by getting out of the car and walking from the front to the rear of the site. Look at the sides of the building as well as its parking area and amenities. Notice the type of tenancy in the building. You can obtain much information by interviewing the resident manager. Form your opinion as to how the sale property compares to the subject in terms of the seven elements of comparison.

CHAPTER TEN

MARKET APPROACH

Through the market approach, value is estimated by analyzing sales and listings of similar properties. Units of comparison are abstracted from other sales and, giving consideration to the seven elements of comparison that are described in the last chapter, these value indicators are applied to the subject property.

The market approach is heavily based on the principle of substitution, which states that a seller will pay no more for a property than the cost of acquiring an equally desirable substitute property. While there has been a recent move to rename this technique the "sales comparison" approach, the FHLMC/FNMA forms and many narrative reports still label it as the market approach.

EXAMPLE 10.1. Abstracting value indicators from a comparable sale

A comparable property you wish to use sold for $1,000,000. At the time of sale it had an annual gross income of $125,000. The property consists of 25 units, 100 rooms, and 20,000 gross square feet. The value indicators are abstracted as follows:

Technique	Abstraction Calculation	Value Indicator
Gross income multiplier:	$1,000,000 / $125,000 =	8.00
Price per unit:	$1,000,000 / 25 units =	$40,000
Price per room:	$1,000,000 / 100 rooms =	$10,000
Price per square foot:	$1,000,000 / 20,000 =	$50.00

Table 10.1. Value Indicators and Abstraction Methods

Value Indicator	Abstraction Method
Gross income multiplier (GIM)	Divide sale price by gross income.
Overall rate (OAR)	Divide net income by sale price. This method is considered a part of the income approach and is discussed in the next chapter.
Price per unit	Divide sales price by number of units.
Price per room	Divide sale price by number of rooms. See Chapter 2 for a discussion of room counts.
Price per square foot	Divide sale price by number of square feet, either gross or rentable. The value indicator must be applied to the corresponding measurement of the subject.

VALUE INDICATORS

For apartment buildings, the market approach consists of five different value indicators (also known as "units of comparison"). You should have enough information on your comparables to abstract all five. Table 10.1 shows this process.

After you have calculated all the comparables' value indicators, make a chart summarizing the indicators. Table 10.2 gives an example for the case study property.

Table 10.2 provides a valuable perspective—in addition to the range of the value indicators, the table quickly shows us the following:

Comparable No. 1

This comparable is the most similar to the subject in terms of unit mix. It should receive special attention for the physical indicators (price per unit, room, and square foot).

Comparable No. 2

With a majority of one-bedroom units, the $51,196 price per unit paid for this property is probably below the subject's corresponding figure, as the subject has mostly two-bedroom units.

Comparable No. 3

This is the most recent sale, and should be analyzed for any indications of recent changes in the market (e.g., high or low gross income multiplier). Is this sale's relatively high GIM proof of an upswing in the market? As noted in Figure 10.1, it appears to be caused by the rents being well below the market level.

Comparable No. 4

Except for the gross income multiplier, which appears suspiciously high, the value indicators for this comparable are below those of the others. If an indicator from the middle of the comparables' range is more appropriate for the subject, this comparable can still be included in order to establish the lower end of the physical indicator range. The possibility of below-market rents at the time of sale could be at least partially responsible for the high GIM—the buyer, seller, or broker should have provided some insight into this situation. Also, the absence of any comment about the high GIM detracts from the credibility of this comparable.

Comparable No. 5

This comparable's physical value indicators are at the high end of the range, and it may help bracket the range of indicators considered appropriate for the subject property. While not indicated in Table 10.2, note that the master-metered utilities have a downward effect on the GIM (due to a greater percentage of income going to pay the utility expenses).

Comparable No. 6

This is not a sale but a current listing, and should be considered only as an indication of the upper end of the market. For example, its gross income multiplier is probably higher than that we'd use for appraising the subject. On the other hand, its units are smaller than the subject's, and the price-per-unit figure we select for the subject may well be higher than Comparable No. 6's asking price of $64,533 per unit. Also, the asking price GIM of 7.93 attaches further suspicion to the 8.10 GIM of Comparable No. 4.

LISTING SALES ON THE 71A FORM

Obviously, the Summary of Sale Comparables (Table 10.2) does not tell the whole story. For instance, it does not note that Comparable No. 2 had received extensive renovation work prior to sale, or that it included a second mortgage carried by the seller at a very low interest rate, and that Sale No. 3 had rents well below those that it could have been achieving. These factors have to be considered in your selection of value indicators to use for the subject property.

Figure 10.1 shows Sale Comparables Nos. 1, 2, and 3 as they are listed on the 71A appraisal form for our case study. The remaining comparables are shown in

Table 10.2. Summary of Sale Comparables

Comparable No.	No. Units	Unit Mix	Sale Date	GIM	OAR	$/Unit	$/Room	$/Sq.Ft.
1	55	2 sgl. 20 1/1 33 2/2	7/88	7.29	8.52%	$66,818	$18,750	$79.31
2	68	50 1/1 18 2/1	1/88	7.49	8.68%	$51,196	$15,682	$67.36
3	40	10 1/1 30 2/2	9/88	7.62	8.14%	$71,250	$19,000	$75.34
4	71	5 sgl. 50 1/1 10 2/1 10 3/2	4/88	8.10	7.78%	$45,070	$12,800	$52.91
5	44	12 1/1 20 2/2 12 3/2	4/88	7.16	8.53%	$72,727	$18,182	$83.12
6	75	50 1/1 25 2/2	listing	7.93	7.78%	$64,533	$19,360	$78.71

MARKET APPROACH

The market data selected are the most recent sales of properties, similar and proximate to subject, knows to the appraiser, that a buyer of subject property would have given consideration to purchasing. In the absence of actual sales, listings of comparable properties may be used but an explanation must be included in the 'Comments' section below.

ITEM	SUBJECT	COMPARABLE NO. 1	COMPARABLE NO. 2	COMPARABLE NO. 3
Address	213 S. Wilson Ave. Metropolis	811 4th Avenue Metropolis	1258 5840th Street Metropolis	1427 22nd Avenue Metropolis
Proximity to Subject		1.8 miles NW	2.5 miles E	4.5 miles S
Map Code	78-F4	63-A5	41-B7	88-C4
Lot Size	22,500/450	25,500/464	34,600/509	21,200/530
Brief Description of Building Improvements	No. Units: 50 No. Vac: 0 Year Built: 19 70 Four story center-court over 2 level sub garage.	No. Units: 55 No. Vac: 2 Year Built: 19 73 Three story cen-tercourt over 1 level sub garage.	No. Units: 68 No. Vac: 4 Year Built: 19 65 Two story side walk-up with detached carports.	No. Units: 40 No. Vac: 2 Year Built: 19 72 Three story cen-tercourt with 1 level sub garage.
Quality	Good	Good	Average	Good
Condition	Average	Average+	Good	Average
Recreational Facilities	Rec room used for storage.	Rec room, sauna.	None	None
Pool	Yes	Yes	Yes	Yes
Parking	Sub garage 1.50/U	Sub garage 1.38/U	Carports 1.00/U	Sub garage 1.50/U
Tenant Appeal	Good	Good	Average	Good
Gross Sq. Ft.	39,585	46,340	51,680	37,828
No. Rooms	178	196	222	150
Security	Full	Full	Pedestrian entries	Full

Unit Breakdown

	SUBJECT				COMPARABLE NO. 1				COMPARABLE NO. 2				COMPARABLE NO. 3			
	No. of Units	UNIT ROOM COUNT Total	BR	Bath	No. of Units	UNIT ROOM COUNT Total	BR	Bath	No. of Units	UNIT ROOM COUNT Total	BR	Bath	No. of Units	UNIT ROOM COUNT Total	BR	Bath
Unit Breakdown	22	3	1	1	2	2	0	1	50	3	1	1	10	3	1	1
	28	4	2	2	20	3	1	1	18	4	2	1	30	4	2	2
					33	4	2	2								

ITEM	SUBJECT	COMPARABLE NO. 1	COMPARABLE NO. 2	COMPARABLE NO. 3
Utilities Paid by Owner	Hot water	Hot water	Hot water	Hot water
Data Source	Inspection, Owner	Lender	Broker, Seller	Appraiser, Buyer
Price	$N/A [x] Unf. [ ] F	$3,675,000 [x] Unf. [ ] F	$3,565,000 [x] Unf. [ ] F	$2,850,000 [x] Unf. [ ] F
Sale - Listing - Offer	Refinance	Sale, Doc 29437	Sale, Doc 14326	Sale Doc 65492
Date of Sale	N/A	July 1988	January 1988	September 1988
Terms (Including conditions of sale and financing terms)	N/A	Cash down:$920,000 (25%) 1st: $2,755,000 (75%) VIR @ 9.5%.	Cash down:$356,500 (10%) 1st: $2,650,000 (74%) VIR @ 9.5%. 2nd:$558,500 (16%) @8%,5 Y's,int.only	Cash down:$725,000 (25%) 1st: $2,125,000 (75%) VIR @ 9.5%.
Complete as many of the following as possible using data effective at time of sale				
Gross Annual Income	$444,300	$504,120	$465,000	$374,005
Gross Ann. Inc. Mult. (1)	N/A	7.29	7.49*	7.62
Net Annual Income	$278,579	$313,059	$302,250	$231,879
Expense Percentage (2)	34.7% + 4% V&CL %	33.9% + 4% V&CL %	31.0% + 4% V&CL %	35% + 3% V&CL %
Overall Cap. Rate (3)	N/A %	8.52 %	8.68* %	8.14 %
Price Per Unit	$N/A	$ 66,818	$ 51,196*	$ 71,250
Price Per Room	$N/A	$ 18,750	$ 15,682*	$ 19,000
Price Gross Bldg. Area	$N/A / sq. ft. bldg. area	$ 79.31 / sq. ft. bldg. area	$ 67.36* / sq. ft. bldg. area	$ 75.34 / sq. ft. bldg. area
COMMENTS		Actual income (above) was close to market level. 2 BR currently rents for $750 to $780.	*Indicators based on cash equivalent price $3,481,309, which reflects 2nd discounted at 12%. 2 BR currently rents for $600.	Market income es-timated by apprsr. is 8.9% above act. (above). Market income GIM is 7.0 2 BR currently rents for $740.
COMPARISON TO SUBJECT		Quality: Similar Condition: Similar Location: Similar	Inferior Similar Similar	Similar Similar Similar Only comp that is master-metered.

VALUE INDICATORS FOR THE SUBJECT PROPERTY		
Indicated Gross Income Multiplier 7.35	X Gross Annual ~~XXXXX~~ Actual Income $444,300	$ 3,265,605
Indicated Value Per Unit $65,000	x 50 Units	$ 3,250,000
Indicated Value Per Room $18,000	x 178 Rooms	$ 3,204,000
Indicated Value Per Sq. Ft. of Gross Bldg. Area $88	x 39,585 Sq. Ft. Bldg. Area	$ 3,483,480
Indicated Overall Capitalization Rate		8.50 %

(1) Sale Price ÷ Gross Annual Income (2) Total Annual Expenses ÷ Total Gross Annual Income (3) Net Annual Income ÷ Price

RECONCILIATION: Comp No. 1 is most similar in respect to design, room count and rent levels, and is given most weight. Comp No. 4 appears to have an unusually high sale price, especially when compared to Comp No. 6, a listing. Most weight given to GIM due to its frequent use by market participants. Secondary weight given to $/unit. Lesser weight given to $/Room and $/Unit. See Page 6b for earnings-ratio adjustments to physical indicators.

INDICATED VALUE BY MARKET APPROACH $3,265,000

Rounded to $3,265,000

FHLMC Form 71A Rev. 8/77 FNMA Form 1050 12/83-1

Page 6 of 8

Figure 10.1. 71A Form showing Sale Comparables Nos. 1, 2 and 3

Figure 10.2. Most appraisers copy the blank page of the appraisal form and use it for listing additional sale comparables. Space on the form is very limited and comments are often abbreviated. Explanations for some of the items are given in Table 10.3.

ADJUSTING FOR CASH EQUIVALENCY

As noted, the second mortgage carried back by the seller of Comparable No. 2 had an interest rate that was below that which the seller would have ordinarily required. Prior to using the comparables to select value indicators for the subject, the cash equivalent sale prices of any such comparables should be calculated—this helps remove the effect that any below-market financing may have had on inflating the price.

SELECTING VALUE INDICATORS

Good judgment and common sense are the key words in the process of selecting value indicators. After reviewing the comparables, select the indicators (either single points or ranges) that you feel are appropriate for the subject. An example of such selections is found in Table 10.4.

Compare the resulting value estimates with each other. They range from \$3,100,000 to \$3,483,480; the final value estimate is somewhere in between. The value estimates must be reanalyzed with respect to each other. For instance, why is the \$/Sq.Ft. indicator conspicuously above the other indicators? Some of the items to consider in refining the range down to a single value estimate are as follows:

1. Which of the indicators is relied upon most by the buyers, sellers, and brokers dealing in the subject's market?
2. Which of the value indicators display the most consistency from one comparable to another?
3. How reliable is the income information obtained for each comparable? How likely is it that erroneous income figures are responsible for a given comparable's especially high or low GIM?
4. How reliable is the square footage figure for each comparable? Could the various room count or square footage figures be based on differing standards or techniques of measurement?
5. Have appeal factors such as location, appearance, management, or tenancy been properly considered in the selection process?
6. Is your income estimate for the subject based on actual or market income? What is the difference between these two? How does this fit in with the sale comparables?

MARKET APPROACH

The market data selected are the most recent sales of properties, similar and proximate to subject, knows to the appraiser, that a buyer of subject property would have given consideration to purchasing. In the absence of actual sales, listings of comparable properties may be used but an explanation must be included in the 'Comments' section below.

ITEM	SUBJECT	COMPARABLE NO. 4	COMPARABLE NO. 5	COMPARABLE NO. 6
Address		2107 28th Avenue Metropolis	5975 Nora Lynn Dr. Metropolis	1027 Pearl Street Metropolis
Proximity to Subject		4 miles S	2.4 miles N	1.6 miles SW
Map Code		88-A6	62-C1	59-E4
Lot Size /SF per unit		32,600/459	50,200/1,141	32,776/437
Brief Description of Building Improvements	No. Units: ___ No. Vac: ___ Year Built: 19	No. Units: 71 No. Vac: NA Year Built: 19 77 Two-story side walk-up with detached carports.	No. Units: 44 No. Vac: 2 Year Built: 19 68 Two-story garden complex with detached carports.	No. Units: 75 No. Vac: 3 Year Built: 19 75 Four-story center court with 2 level sub garage.
Quality		Average	Good	Good
Condition		Average	Good	Average
Recreational Facilities		Rec room	Rec room, tennis court, sauna	Rec room, sauna
Pool		Yes	Pool and spa	Yes
Parking		Carports 1.50/U	Caports 1.61/U	Sub garage 1.50/U
Tenant Appeal		Average	Good	Good
Security		None	Full	Full
No. Rooms		250	176	250
No. Sq. Ft.		60,485	38,500	61,490
Unit Breakdown (No. of Units: Unit Room Count Total / BR / Bath)	No. of Units; Unit Room Count: Total, BR, Bath	5: 2 / 0 / 1 50: 3 / 1 / 1 10: 4 / 2 / 1 10: 5 / 3 / 2	12: 3 / 1 / 1 20: 4 / 2 / 2 12: 5 / 3 / 2	50: 3 / 1 / 1 25: 4 / 2 / 2
Utilities Paid by Owner		Hot water	All	Hot water
Data Source		Lender	Appraiser, Seller	Listing broker
Price	$ ☐ Unf. ☐ F	$ 3,200,000 ☒ Unf. ☐ F	$ 3,200,000 ☒ Unf. ☐ F	$4,840,000 ☒ Unf. ☐ F
Sale - Listing - Offer		Sale, Doc 21068	Sale, Doc 20963	LISTING
Date of Sale		April 1988	April 1988	Listed 8-4-88
Terms (including conditions of sale and financing terms)		Cash down:$320,000 (10%). 1st: $2,400,000 (75%) new VIR. 2nd:$480,000 (15%) @ 13%, 5 years.	Cash down:$640,000 (20%) 1st: $2,560,000 (80%) VIR @ 9.5%.	Buyer to obtain new 1st. Seller may carry small, short-term 2nd.
Complete as many of the following as possible using data effective at time of sale				
Gross Annual Income	$	$ 395,060	$ 446,825	$ 610,340
Gross Ann. Inc. Mult. (1)		8.10	7.16	7.93
Net Annual Income	$	$ 248,890	$ 272,966	$ 376,588
Expense Percentage (2)	%	33.0% + 4% V&CL %	34.9% + 4% V&CL %	34.3% + 4% V&CL %
Overall Cap. Rate (3)	%	7.78 %	8.53 %	7.78 %
Price Per Unit	$	$ 45,070	$ 72,727	$ 64,533
Price Per Room	$	$ 12,800	$ 18,182	$ 19,360
Price Gross Bldg. Area	$ / sq. ft. bldg. area	$ 52.91 / sq. ft. bldg. area	$ 83.12 / sq. ft. bldg. area	$ 78.71 / sq. ft. bldg. area
COMMENTS		2 BR currently rents for $640. 2nd mortgage is considered to be at market terms.	Master-metered for utilities. 2BR currently rents for $770-$800. Only comp that is master-metered.	This is a current listing and is used to indicate the top of the value range. 2BR rents for $750.
COMPARISON TO SUBJECT		Quality: Inferior Condition: Inferior Location: Similar Overall: Inferior	Similar Similar Similar Similar	Similar Similar Similar Similar

Page 6a

Figure 10.2. Modified page from 71A Form showing Sale Comparables Nos. 4, 5 and 6

Table 10.3. Explanations for Some Items on 71A Appraisal Form

Row	Comment
Lot size	Following the lot size is the square feet of land per unit (lot size divided by number of units). This allows for a comparison of density.
Parking	The "1.XX/u" figure refers to the number of parking spaces per unit (total parking spaces divided by number of units).
Unit breakdown	For the lay reader, the unit room count (e.g. 3-1-1) can add confusion and make the breakdown undecipherable. Again, a 3-1-1 is a one-bedroom one bath, a 4-2-2 is a two-bedroom two-bath, and so forth. A more complete discussion of room counts is provided in Chapter 2.
Sale-listing-offer	The "Doc" number refers to the document number given by the county recorder to the conveyance deed. This has been included to note the appraiser's verification that the transaction has actually closed.
Terms	Federal and state regulators of lending institutions have become more adamant about appraisers providing the financing terms behind the sale. As in the case of Comparable No. 2, below-market financing can result in an artificially high sale price, and a cash equivalency adjustment should be made. Enough financing information should be included so that the reader can do his or her own cash equivalency calculation.
Expense percentage	The "V&CL" figure is the amount of vacancy and collection loss reflected in the net income figure. More often (although this may not be as desirable), appraisers state expenses and V&CL as a single figure.
Comments	Providing the current rental figures for the comparables gives a means for comparing their overall appeal to that of the subject. Any indication of below-market income should be included here, as should any other information that is not included elsewhere but which affects your analysis.

Table 10.4. Value Indicators in the Market Approach

Technique	Selection	Value Indication
GIM	7.25 GIM × $444,300 = 7.50 GIM × $444,300 =	$3,221,175 $3,332,250
$/Unit	50 units × $62,000 50 units × $68,000	$3,100,000 $3,400,000
$/Room	178 rooms × $17,500	$3,115,000
$/Room	178 rooms × $18,500	$3,293,000
$/Sq.Ft.	39,585 sq.ft. × $88	$3,483,480

Your report should include a discussion of your selection process. As a reviewer of appraisal reports I find that, upon being questioned, appraisers often verbally describe a different selection process than that which they've described in their reports. The verbal description is generally more sensible and supportive of their selection, while what they've actually written is more general and traditional

Table 10.5. Subject/Indicators Interplay

Property Characteristic	General Rules for Selecting Value Indicators
Subject has low rents in relation to the market level; sale comparables have rents closer to market (assume actual rents are used in the appraisal)	Use a high GIM
Subject rents are at the top of the market. Comparable rents are at the middle or lower part of the market	Use a low GIM
Subject's average number of rooms per unit is below that of the comparables	Use a lower $/Unit figure and a higher $/Room figure
Subject shows signs of mismanagement and an undesirable tennancy	Use lower GIM and physical indicators
Subject has few amenities and generally less appeal	Use lower GIM and physical indicators
Subject is of high quality	Use higher GIM and physical indicators
Subject's neighborhood is less desirable than that of the comparables	Use lower GIM and physical indicators

("boiler plate"). As long as the selection process makes sense, it needn't follow traditions or be too academic.

Table 10.5 shows some general rules regarding the interplay between the characteristics of the subject property and the selection of indicators for that subject.

ADJUSTING THE PHYSICAL INDICATORS

A pure application of the price-per-unit indicator assumes that the units in both the subject and comparables have the same income potential. However, a building with 10 two-bedroom units will sell for more than a building with 10 one-bedroom units (all else being equal); to make a direct comparison between the two, using this indicator, is invalid. The problem becomes more serious when one realizes that the subject and comparables will rarely, if ever, have identical unit mixes. This problem can be dealt with by adjusting the physical value indicators, using the earnings ratio adjustment technique. Example 10.2 illustrates this.

EXAMPLE 10.2. Using the Earnings Ratio Adjustment Technique

Comparable No. 2 in our case study sold for a cash equivalent price of $51,196 per unit. The average rent per unit for the subject and the comparable are as follows:

Subject's average monthly rent per unit:	$740.50
Comparable No. 2 average monthly rent per unit:	$569.85

Once you've determined these figures, find the income ratio of the subject rent per unit to that of the comparable:

$$\frac{\text{Subject average rent per unit}}{\text{Comparable average rent per unit}} = \frac{\$740.50}{\$569.85} = 1.30$$

The resulting figure is the ratio of the subject's average rent per unit to that of the comparable. In other words, the subject's average rent per unit is 1.30 times that of the comparable.

The adjusted price per unit is found by multiplying the comparable's dollar sale price per unit by the above factor:

$$\$51{,}196 \times 1.30 = \$66{,}555$$

The subject's number of units multiplied by this amount results in a subject property value indication of $3,327,750 (50 × $66,555).

DOLLARS PER UNIT

Property	Sale Price/ Unit	Gross Income Unit/Mo.	Adjustment Factor	Adjusted $/Unit
SUBJECT		$741		
Comp #l	$66,818	$764	0.97	$64,778
Comp #2	$51,196	$570	1.30	$66,527
Comp #3	$71,250	$779	0.95	$67,713
Comp #4	$45,070	$464	1.60	$71,977
Comp #5	$72,727	$846	0.88	$63,638
Comp #6	$64,533	$678	1.09	$70,466
	$61,932	< AVERAGES >	1.13	$67,517

DOLLARS PER ROOM

Property	Sale Price/ Room	Gross Income Room/Mo.	Adjustment Factor	Adjusted $/Room
SUBJECT		$208		
Comp #l	$18,750	$214	0.97	$18,196
Comp #2	$15,682	$175	1.19	$18,687
Comp #3	$19,000	$208	1.00	$19,021
Comp #4	$12,800	$132	1.58	$20,218
Comp #5	$18,182	$212	0.98	$17,876
Comp #6	$19,360	$203	1.02	$19,794
	$17,296	< AVERAGES >	1.12	$18,965

DOLLARS PER SQUARE FOOT

Property	Sale Price/ Square Foot	Gross Income Sq.Ft./Mo.	Adjustment Factor	Adjusted $/Sq.Ft.
SUBJECT		$0.94		
Comp #l	$79.31	$0.91	1.03	$81.82
Comp #2	$67.36	$0.75	1.25	$84.03
Comp #3	$75.34	$0.82	1.14	$85.53
Comp #4	$52.91	$0.54	1.72	$90.91
Comp #5	$83.12	$0.97	0.97	$80.38
Comp #6	$78.71	$0.83	1.13	$89.01
	$72.79	< AVERAGES >	1.21	$85.28

Figure 10.3. Adjustment grid for physical value indicators

A similar adjustment can be made with the dollars-per-room and dollars-per-square-foot indicators, with the adjustment ratio merely computed on the average rent per room or rent per square foot. One possible way of formating this technique for the report is shown in Figure 10.3, in which adjustments are made for the six sale comparables used in the case study. The calculation of this adjustment is ideally suited for a personal computer with a spreadsheet program. If nothing else, knowing whether the earnings ratio is positive or negative is of help when selecting the appropriate physical indicators for the subject. Note that the calculations in Figure 10.3 were performed by computer, resulting in slightly different answers than those obtained through manual calculations (due to rounding).

RECONCILING THE VALUE INDICATORS INTO A SINGLE ESTIMATE

The four value indicators have resulted in four separate value estimates. The value estimates selected for our case study are as follows (The selection and subsequent value estimate calculation can be seen on the lower part of the appraisal form shown in Figure 10.1):

Gross income multiplier:	$3,265,605
Value per unit:	$3,250,000
Value per room:	$3,204,000
Value per square foot:	$3,483,480

A single value estimate must be selected. This estimate may be selected from anywhere within the indicated range, and is generally rounded. The selection process depends largely on the appropriateness and accuracy of each approach. Also, consistency among value indicators should be considered. For instance, if the GIMs form a tight range and the physical indicators are more spread-out, the value based on the GIM may be given more consideration.

Buyers and sellers in many markets place primary emphasis on the gross income multiplier. This by itself favors the value estimate as indicated by the GIM. The physical indicators can be more difficult for investors to work with, especially if comparable sales and listings have varying unit mixes. The sales-price-per-square-foot indicator is usually given the least weight due to inconsistencies in measuring methods and unavailability of square footage figures to buyers and sellers.

In the case study, most weight is given to the GIM, and a value of $3,265,000 is chosen as the indicated value by the market approach. A last check of this value shows that it is well supported by the other methods, as well:

$3,265,000 = 7.35 GIM
$65,300 per unit
$18,343 per room
$82.48 per square foot

CHAPTER ELEVEN

INCOME APPROACH

This approach is very similar to using the gross income multiplier, but with two distinct differences: (1) a *capitalization rate* is used in place of the multiplier, and (2) the rate is *divided into net income* rather than multiplied against the gross income.

As the income approach uses net income rather than gross income to measure value, it is considered by many to be more refined than the market approach (at least for larger income-producing properties) and is often given most weight in the final reconciliation. On the surface, two advantages appear to favor the income approach: (1) the capitalization rate can be derived in several ways, and (2) the net income figure is more refined than the gross income figure.

CONCEPT OF THE OVERALL RATE

The capitalization rate (also known as the "overall rate") is a rate of return. It is the percentage of sale price or value that is received annually as net income. Conversely, dividing this rate into net income gives us a value estimate.

USING THE OVERALL RATE TO ESTIMATE THE SUBJECT PROPERTY'S VALUE

While this chapter focuses on a number of methods for deriving the overall rate, the OAR's real usefulness is in its application to the subject property.

EXAMPLE 11.1 Estimating the subject's value with the OAR

The subject property in our case study has a net income of $277,588. After careful analysis of the sale comparables, we select an overall rate of 8.50 percent to apply to the subject property. Our value estimate is calculated by dividing net income by the overall rate:

$277,588 / .085 = $3,265,741

The overall rate at which a property sells for is greatly affected by its risk, liquidity, and management profile. An investor purchasing a risky property with intensive management will require a higher rate of return (which results in a lower value). On the other hand, with less risk and less management involvement, the investor will probably settle for a smaller income in relation to purchase price. As such, the OAR bears an inverse relationship to value: the higher the OAR, the lower the price or value estimate. As will be shown later in this chapter, financing also has an effect on the overall rate. A more detailed discussion of how risk, liquidity, and management affect rates of return can be found in Chapter 16.

DERIVING THE OVERALL RATE FROM COMPARABLE SALES

The most traditional and widely used method for estimating the overall rate is to abstract it from comparable sales; this is very similar to the way in which the GIM is abstracted. The OAR is abstracted from a comparable sale by dividing its net income by its sale price.

EXAMPLE 11.2. Abstracting an overall rate from a comparable sale

In our case study, Comparable No. 1 sold for $3,675,000. Its annual net income is $313,059. Its overall rate is calculated as follows:

$313,059 / $3,675,000 = .0852 (or 8.52%)

Selecting the overall rate requires the same sort of review of the comparables as was shown in the selection of sale comparables chapter (Chapter 9). The only two items that are included in the overall rate but not included in the gross income multiplier are 1) operating expenses and 2) vacancy and collection loss. Therefore, the selection analysis follows the same approach as is used for the gross income multiplier. In fact, Paul Gilon, MAI refers to the sale-abstracted overall rate as the "net income divider," and considers it to belong to the market approach rather than to the income approach.

All other things being equal, if the subject has higher expense and vacancy ratios than the comparables, the appropriate overall rate is higher. If the subject has a lower expense and vacancy ratio, the appropriate OAR is lower.

OTHER METHODS IN THE INCOME APPROACH

While abstracting the overall rate from comparable sales is usually the preferred method, there are additional ways of estimating overall rates and value in the income approach. The most popular and applicable methods are as follows:

1. Overall rate derivation through the band-of-investment technique
2. Overall rate derivation through the debt coverage ratio technique
3. Equity residual technique
4. Overall rate derivation through one of the Ellwood techniques

While these methods are considered by many appraisal users as being unacceptable alternatives to the abstraction method, their discussion provides a good insight into the overall rate and its relationship to financing and equity return. The first three methods are discussed in the following paragraphs, using our case study as an example. The Ellwood method is excluded from discussion here, as it is used relatively little in apartment appraisals and requires lengthy math calculations.

OVERALL RATE DERIVATION THROUGH THE BAND-OF-INVESTMENT

An overall rate can be calculated if certain information is available about financing and investors' cashflow expectations. The required variables for this technique are

1. Loan-to-value ratio (as a percentage)
2. Equity-to-value ratio (as a percentage)
3. Annual loan constant (annual payments expressed as a percentage of the loan amount)
4. Investor's expected cash flow rate (annual before-tax return required by the investor on the equity portion of the investment)

The *loan-to-value ratio* and interest rate should reflect that readily obtainable in the market, and should not reflect unusually favorable terms that might be available from one specific seller willing to carry back a loan. This information should be available by surveying local institutional lenders. The interest rate will often vary according to the general quality of the property.

Equity is the cash portion of the purchase price. Because the purchase price is composed of loan and equity, their ratios together will total 100 percent: If the loan-to-value ratio is 75 percent, then the equity-to-value ratio is 25 percent.

The *annual loan constant* is the percentage of the loan amount paid by the borrower to the lender in annual payments. It is calculated by dividing the loan amount into the annual loan payment. However, at this juncture the value and loan amount for the subject property may still not be known. The constant may still be determined by dividing any loan amount by its annual payment. Whether you use a financial calculator or tables, the simplest way to figure the annual constant is to figure the loan payment for one dollar. This figure is the loan constant. For example, if the interest rate is 9.5 percent and the amortization period is 360 months, the annual payment is $0.1009 (12 times the monthly payment of $0.00841), and the loan constant is 0.1009. See Calculator Procedure No. 1 (Appendix B) for directions on calculating the annual loan constant.

The *cashflow rate* is an investor's expected or required annual rate of return on his or her equity investment. This is sometimes called the cash-on-cash return. It is most reliably abstracted from sale comparables. However, you'll also do well to query brokers and investors about their opinions of what the expected and/or required cashflow rate should be for a specific property. For instance, in the Los Angeles market as of this writing, cashflow rates range from 0 percent (loan payments precisely equaling net income) to 8 percent, depending on the quality of the investment (better properties having lower cash-flow requirements) and the amount of the downpayment. Smaller properties often sell at a negative cashflow, the investor betting on tax shelter and appreciation to provide an acceptable rate of return. If a particular property within their market was described to them, the cashflow rates suggested by most brokers and investors would probably be within a few percentage points of each other.

Having now obtained the necessary four numbers we are now ready to use them in the band-of-investment calculation. We'll assume that a cashflow rate of 4.0 percent has been selected.

Loan-to-value ratio × annual constant	.75 × .1009 = .0757
Equity ratio × cashflow rate	.25 × .0400 = .0100
Overall Rate	= .0857
	(or 8.57%)

Value = $278,579 NOI / .0857 = $3,250,630

EXAMPLE 11.3. Abstracting cashflow rates from comparables

Comparable Sale No. 1 sold for $3,675,000 and had a net income of $313,059. It was financed for $2,755,000 (75 percent of purchase price) at a rate of 9.50 percent, with an amortization period of 360 months.

To calculate the cashflow rate:

Step 1

Determine annual loan payments:

Calculator Procedure No. 1 shows the annual loan payment to be $277,986.

Step 2

Find the amount of cashflow to the equity position:

Deducting the $277,986 annual payment from the $313,059 annual net income leaves a $35,073 cash flow to the equity position.

Step 3

Determine the equity investment:

Deducting financing of $2,755,000 from the $3,675,000 purchase price results in an equity investment of $920,000.

Step 4

Divide annual cashflow by the equity amount in order to determine the cashflow rate:

$$\$35,073 / \$920,000 = .0381 \quad \text{(or 3.81\%)}$$

OVERALL RATE DERIVATION THROUGH THE DEBT COVERAGE RATIO TECHNIQUE

Lenders use the debt coverage ratio (DCR) to determine the maximum they can loan on a property. They divide the property's net income figure by their debt coverage ratio in a two-step process that tells them how much they can lend.

A lender typically may use a DCR of between 1.00 and 1.25 to ensure that the property will provide at least enough cashflow; A DCR of 1.00 is obviously a break-even cashflow; a DCR of less than 1.00 means that the net income is insufficient to cover the loan payments, and a DCR over 1.00 provides a safety cushion for the lender.

The following exercise of determining maximum loan amount is provided to demonstrate what a DCR is—next we'll use it to derive an overall rate which reflects a purchaser willing to put down 25 percent and take the biggest mortgage possible. Assume the same 9.5 percent, 30-year loan as used in the previous examples. The required information consists of the DCR, the loan-to-value ratio, and annual constant. All of the numbers are included in a multiplication equation which results in the OAR.

This overall rate is based solely on financing information, and assumes that an investor would purchase a property based on obtaining a typical institutional loan. If the property would not provide enough cashflow under this arrangement to be

---

EXAMPLE 11.4. Using the debt coverage ratio to determine a maximum loan amount

Metropolis Savings Bank is asked to quote their biggest and best loan for the case study property. The property has a net income of $278,579. Metropolis is currently using a debt coverage ratio of 1.15. Their loan terms for the subject are a 9.50 percent interest rate with monthly payments completely amortizing the loan over 30 years.

Step 1

Divide the property's net income by the debt coverage ratio.

$$\$278{,}579 \,/\, 1.15 = \$242{,}243$$

The result is the maximum amount of net income that the lender can take for monthly payments.

Step 2

The product from above is then divided by the loan constant.

$$\$242{,}243 \,/\, 0.1009 = \$2{,}400{,}823$$

The maximum loan is $2,400,000 (lenders always round down).

EXAMPLE 11.5. Using the DCR to derive an overall rate

The required information is as follows:

Debt Coverage Ratio	1.15
Loan-to-Value Ratio	75%
Annual Constant	0.1009

The numbers are multiplied together to obtain the overall rate.

$1.15 \times .75 \times 0.1009 = 0.0870$ (or 8.70%)

Value = \$278,579 NOI / .0870 = \$3,202,057

saleable, the appropriate overall rate is higher than that derived through the debt coverage method. The resulting cashflow rate can be calculated as follows:

OAR:	.0870
Financing: .75 × .1009 =	− .0757
Equity portion of OAR:	.0113

.0113 / .25 cashflow rate = 0.0452, or a 4.5% cashflow rate

Note that the debt coverage method of estimating an overall rate is very sensitive to the selected debt coverage ratio; replacing the 1.15 DCR with 1.10 would result in an overall rate of 8.32 percent.

USING THE EQUITY RESIDUAL TECHNIQUE TO ESTIMATE VALUE

This technique is most closely related to the debt coverage valuation technique. It is based on the premise that the value of a property is the combined amount of the loan(s) and the equity position. Depending on how a property would likely be financed, either the existing loan can be used, or a new loan can be computed using the same techniques as previously discussed. The value of the equity position is computed as the cashflow divided by the cashflow rate. As such, this technique provides an estimate more of investment value rather than of market value. An example follows.

Note that this method is very sensitive to the selected cashflow rate. For instance, using a 2 percent cashflow rate would result in a value of \$4,220,650.

EXAMPLE 11.6. Calculations of the Equity Residual Technique

The subject property has an annual net income of $278,579. The most attractive financing program is an institutional loan of $2,400,000 with annual payments of $242,166, leaving a cashflow of $36,413. The cashflow rate required by an investor is 4.0 percent. The resulting value of the equity position is $910,325 ($36,413 / .040 = $910,325). Summing the loan amount and the equity value results in a value estimate:

Amount of loan =	$2,400,000
Value of equity position =	910,325
Value estimate =	$3,310,325
Round to:	$3,300,000

NET INCOME PITFALLS IN THE INCOME APPROACH

Hardly a day goes by without someone telephoning me for a recommendation about what cap rate to use for a certain property. I always tell them that due to differing opinions about operating expenses and vacancy rates, I'm more comfortable talking about gross income multipliers. In the same vein, when using comparables to abstract overall rates, one is very reliant on the comparables' vacancy and expense figures being accurate; obtaining accurate expense figures is very difficult. Consider the following situations:

1. If the comparable's expense figure is based on historical figures, these may reflect excessive expenses which result from a capital improvement program, unusual turn-over, and so on.
2. Historical figures may be low, due to the owner's neglect of maintenance or management duties.
3. Historical figures may be skewed due to either insufficient or excessive management fees.
4. Brokers will often underestimate the true cost of running a property, and their expense figures may be too low.
5. If the expense figures are obtained from another appraiser, that individual's estimation techniques may be different than yours, or reflect a different style of management.

Almost all market-derived overall rates are subject to the above aberrations. Hence, using an overall rate may convolute the value estimation process rather than refine it. For this reason, I often prefer the market approach to the income approach. Luckily, I work in a market with a large amount of comparable sales—not everyone has this luxury.

A WORD ABOUT INVESTMENT VALUE

Market value refers to the price a property will bring when exposed to various buyers. Investment value is the value to a particular individual. When selling a property, the seller will most often determine the listing and selling price by using the market approach. Buyers, on the other hand, often use the market approach in conjunction with an equity residual technique in determining what they'll pay for a property. While the previously discussed methods (market approach and capitalization rate) are usually the appraiser's most reliable methods for estimating market value, the methodologies used by investors are an important part of market pricing and should not go without discussion.

Each of the three tiers of investors described in Chapter 1 attacks the pricing problem a little differently. The first two tiers, mom-and-pops and mid-level buyers, generally start with a certain amount of cash for the downpayment. Their posture is often one of "We have two hundred thousand dollars and want to buy an apartment building." In looking for a property which will fit this downpayment limitation, the investor or good broker might go through the following process:

1. Find a property which is fairly priced, can be purchased with the available downpayment, and fits the investor's needs with regard to risk and management requirements. Note that the determination of whether a property is fairly priced is usually, at least at this point, based on experience, minimal comparable sales, and relatively quick judgment—not an in-depth appraisal process such as is described in this book.
2. Then consider the financing. Many properties are priced to require new financing. Using the property's estimated net income, the applicable debt coverage ratio, and other loan parameters, the broker or investor will estimate the maximum amount of financing which can be placed on the property. This may include a second mortgage to be carried back by the seller. The lender of the first loan may set certain limitations on the amount of any secondary financing, such as disallowing payments so great as to cause a negative cashflow.
3. Add the amount of the downpayment and financing to determine the price that might be paid for the property.

4. Compare this offering price to the listing price and market value of the property. Before any offer is presented, the two amounts should be close enough that an agreement between buyer and seller is considered possible. Obviously, the buyer doesn't want to pay more than market value; a more detailed appraisal process may be undertaken at this time.

You'll note the similarity between the above process and the equity residual technique discussed in this chapter. The estimate of market value is used more as a limitation on offering price.

The upper tier of purchasers (financial institutions, Japanese entities, public limited partnerships) use a variety of purchase price determinants. They are often more flexible with regard to downpayment and may base decisions on capitalization rate and internal rate of return requirements (IRR is discussed in Chapter 16). These types of investors may deal in such large geographic areas that they cannot keep track of market values. In these cases, a preliminary determination of the possible offering price will probably precede any expensive appraisal work.

CHAPTER TWELVE

RECONCILIATION

When more than one approach to value is used and the indications are different, it is necessary to reconcile the values into a single estimate of value. The approaches are judged in accordance with the following criteria:

1. Appropriateness of the approach
2. Accuracy of the approach
3. Quantity and quality of evidence

COST APPROACH

The cost approach is usually given the least weight. This can occur even when the property is new, but there are abundant sales to better support the market approach value. Also, investors often do not consider development as an acceptable alternative to purchasing an operating apartment complex. This is especially true for small investors and, because of this, the cost approach might be inappropriate. In smaller or inactive markets the cost approach may be given more consideration. More commentary about the applicability of the cost approach is provided in Chapter 1.

MARKET APPROACH

The more good sales comparables you have, the greater the weight which is placed on this approach. A metropolitan area providing a sufficient number of good sales for this valuation approach is a clear case where the market approach is often given most weight. The market approach sees additional popularity for smaller "ma-and-pa"-type properties.

If you are working where the comparables date back to different market conditions, you'll have to consider in what direction values have gone and how far. This is a time to reconsider the sales comparables: How recent are they? What's happened to mortgage interest rates and other facets of the market since the sales occurred? Do you have adequate financing details for the comparables? How do they compare to the subject in location? How do they compare in size? How accurate and reliable is the information? At this point, you should have no uncertainties about the data.

INCOME APPROACH

There are fewer investors for larger properties, and the investors can often be somewhat more selective about specific return requirements (e.g., overall rate, internal rate of return) being met. In such cases the income approach closely follows the market's rationale for setting prices. The income approach receives additional emphasis when there is insufficient information on the comparable sales.

Which method did you use for deriving the overall rate? If you used abstraction, how certain are you about the reliability of the comparables' operating expenses and net income? If these are at all suspect, should the gross income multiplier in the market approach be given more weight instead?

Chapter 11 discusses the applicability of the income approach to buyers. Does your value estimate represent a purchase price that could be financed and result in a loan-to-value ratio and cashflow rate similar to those of your sales comparables? If not, why not? As noted in Chapter 11, an 8.50 percent overall rate was abstracted from the comparable sales and applied to the subject. Also in that chapter, the debt coverage ratio technique resulted in an 8.70 percent overall rate. The band-of-investment technique resulted in an overall rate of 8.57 percent. Simple computations show that the DCR technique would result in the 8.50 percent capitalization rate if 1) the debt coverage ratio was lowered to 1.12, or 2) if the loan-to-value ratio was lowered to 73 percent.* Does this make sense when considering the property and the current market?

*(1) overall rate / annual loan constant / loan-to-value ratio = debt coverage ratio:

$$\frac{.085}{.1009 \,/\, .75} = 1.12$$

(2) overall rate / annual loan constant / debt coverage ratio = loan-to-value ratio:

$$\frac{.085}{.1009 \,/\, 1.15} = 73\%$$

RECONCILIATION AND VALUE CONCLUSION

Indicated Value by the Cost Approach .... $

Indicated Value by the Market Approach $3,265,000

Indicated Value by the Income Approach $3,275,000

FINAL RECONCILIATION Least weight given to Cost Approach due to difficulty of estimating reproduction cost and accrued depreciation. Also, if vacant, only 37 units could be reproduced on the subject site.

Substantial weight given to Market Approach due to abundance of good sale comparables.

Secondary weight given to Income Approach: Primary weakness is in estimate of expenses for comparables. Both the Market and Income Approaches Support the final estimate of value.

CONDITIONS AND REQUIREMENTS OF APPRAISAL (include required repairs, replacements, painting, termite inspections, etc.) No special conditions or requirements. Property is appraised in as-is condition.

Subject property was last sold in October 1983 for $2,300,000, cash to a new loan.

VALUATION: This Appraisal is based upon the definition of Market Value, the Certification, the Contingent and Limiting Conditions, and the requirements that are stated in this report.

As a result of my investigation and analysis, my estimate of Market Value of the subject property as of October 29, 1988 is..........

$ 3,265,000

Date ______ Appraiser ______

If Applicable, complete the following

Date ______ Appraiser ______

Date ______ ☐ Supervising or ☐ Review Appraiser ______

☐ Did ☐ Did not physically inspect property.

CERTIFICATION: The Appraiser certifies and agrees that

1. The Appraiser has no present or contemplated future interest in the property appraised and neither the employment to make this Appraisal, nor the compensation for it, is contingent upon the appraised value of the property.
2. The Appraiser has no personal interest in or bias with respect to the subject matter of the appraisal report or the participants to the sale. The 'Estimate of Market Value' in the appraisal report is not based in whole or in part upon the race, color, or national origin of the prospective owners or occupants of the property appraised, or upon the race, color, or national origin of present owners or occupants of the properties in the vicinity of the property appraised.
3. The Appraiser has personally inspected the property, both inside and out, and has made an exterior inspection of all comparable sales listed herein. To the best of the Appraiser's knowledge and belief, all statements and information in this report are true and correct, and the Appraiser has not knowingly withheld any significant information.
4. All contingent and limiting conditions are contained herein (imposed by the terms of the assignment or by the undersigned affecting the analyses, opinions, and conclusions contained in this report).
5. This Appraisal Report has been made in conformity with and is subject to the requirements of the Code of Professional Ethics and Standards of Professional Conduct of the appraisal organizations with which the Appraiser is affiliated.
6. All conclusions and opinions concerning the real estate that are set forth in the Appraisal Report were prepared by the Appraiser whose signature appears above on this Appraisal Report, unless indicated as 'Review Appraiser.' No changes of any item of the Appraisal Report shall be made by anyone other than the Appraiser, and the Appraiser shall have no responsibility for any such unauthorized change.

CONTINGENT AND LIMITING CONDITIONS: The certification of the Appraiser appearing in this Appraisal Report is subject to the following conditions and to such other specific and limiting conditions as are set forth by the Appraiser in the report.

1. The Appraiser assumes no responsibility for matters of a legal nature affecting the property appraised or the title thereto, nor does the Appraiser render any opinion as to the title, which is assumed to be good and marketable. The property is appraised as though under responsible ownership.
2. Any sketch in this report may show approximate dimensions and is included to assist the reader in visualizing the property. The Appraiser has made no survey of the property.
3. The Appraiser is not required to give testimony or appear in court because of having made this Appraisal with reference to the property in question, unless arrangments have been previously made therefor.
4. The distribution of the total valuation in this report between land and improvements applies only under the existing program of utilization. The separate valuations for land and building must not be used in conjunction with any other Appraisal and are invalid if so used.
5. The Appraiser assumes that there are no hidden or unapparent conditions of the property, subsoil, or structures which would render it more or less valuable. The Appraiser assumes no responsibility for such conditions or for engineering which might be required to discover such factors.
6. Information, estimates, and opinions furnished to the Appraiser, and contained in this report, were obtained from sources considered reliable and believed to be true and correct. However, no responsibility for accuracy of such items furnished the Appraiser can be assumed by the Appraiser.
7. Disclosure of the contents of this Appraisal Report is governed by the By-laws and Regulations of the professional appraiser organizations with which the Appraiser is affiliated.
8. Neither all nor any part of the contents of this report, or copy thereof (including conclusions as to property value, the identity of the Appraiser, professional designations, referenced to any professional appraisal organizations, or the firm with which the Appraiser is connected) shall be used for any purposes by anyone but the client shown on Page 1 of this report, the mortgagee or its successors and assigns, mortgage insurers, consultants, professional appraisal organizations any state or federally approved financial institution, any department agency, or instrumentality of the United States or of any State or of the District of Columbia, without the previous written consent of the Appraiser; nor shall it be conveyed by anyone to the public through advertising, public relations, news, sales, or other media, without the written consent and approval of the Appraiser.
9. On all Appraisals involving proposed construction, the Appraisal Report and value conclusion are contingent upon completion of the proposed improvements in accordance with the plans and specifications prepared by ______ with a last revision date of ______ which has been initialed and dated by the Appraiser.

FHLMC Form 71A Rev. 8/77 FNMA Form 1050 12/83-1

Figure 11.1. Final reconciliation section of 71A Report

THE FINAL SELECTION

This step should only be taken when you've reconsidered each approach for reliability and appropriateness. At this point, you should have a good feeling of confidence about at least one of the approaches. Once you've picked a final value estimate, compute the resulting value indicators. If, for instance, you've selected the income approach value, the resulting gross income multiplier and physical approaches should be within reason. For instance, an 8.25 percent overall rate may appear reasonable in itself, but the sale comparables may indicate that the value estimate should be above the resulting $66,000 per unit. The reason(s) for such inconsistencies should be discussed in the reconciliation section of the report. Finally, when two approaches both show good support, it is common practice to select a value figure somewhere in between.

Figure 12.1 shows a completed Final Reconciliation section from the 71A report. While every appraisal should have a list of assumptions and limiting conditions, any that are unusual or especially important should be clearly stated with the value conclusion as well as in the transmittal letter.

ROUNDING

How closely to round depends on your confidence in the value. Most reviewers would be suspicious of a value estimate of $2,142,500—markets are not that perfect, and most appraisals lack the evidence to call a value that close. A figure of $2,150,000 would reflect a little more realism. While most appraisal assignments call for the value estimate as a single point, a range may be desirable if the purpose of the appraisal is to advise an owner who is considering selling the property. Be sure to state what the extremes of the range represent: What is your level of confidence? How long will the marketing period most likely be?

CHAPTER THIRTEEN

CASH EQUIVALENCE

The potential sale price for the same property may vary over a wide range because of the variety of available purchase financing. If a property is to be used as a comparable sale and has sold for an inflated price because of some form of favorable financing, some adjustment must be made to the price before a fair comparison can be made to the subject property. This brief chapter offers techniques for adjusting comparable sales for favorable financing.

ADJUSTING A COMPARABLE SALE

The need for using the first two techniques arises when a comparable is sold with financing that does not conform to the current market's interest rate or financing structure. For instance, a property would probably sell for two different prices depending on which of the two following financing arrangements could be contracted:

Alternative A

Assumable 8.50 percent loan for 75 percent of sale price, seller to provide secondary financing for 15 percent of sale price at 10 percent interest only, all due and payable at the end of 10 years.

Alternative B

75 percent conventional loan at 11 percent interest per annum, amortized over 30 years, 25 percent cash down.

This chapter is taken from *Apartment Building Valuation, Financing and Investment Analysis* (John Wiley & Sons, 1982).

With the favorable financing under Alternative A (more leverage and lower interest), the seller could ask more and the purchaser would pay more than with the conventional financing under Alternative B. It is necessary to find what amount of value this favorable financing adds before using such a sale as a comparable. Otherwise the units of comparison (gross rent multiplier, overall rate, and the physical methods) may indicate an artificially high value, reflecting the benefit of financing not necessarily available to the subject property.

The cash equivalence technique provides a method of reducing a comparable's sale price to compensate for favorable financing terms. The comparable sale is repriced with currently available interest rates. The source for typical rates most likely would be an institutional lender or other third party loaning money to the general public at the going rate. Adjusting comparables to market financing is considered the same as adjusting to a cash basis, because a market-rate loan theoretically could be sold for cash to a financial institution or other loan purchaser without any discount off the face value of the loan. Therefore, a loan at the current market rate is already at its cash equivalence and no adjustment need be made.

In essence, the cash equivalence technique might tell us that the comparable that sold for $1,000,000 with favorable financing might have sold for only $925,000 if the owner hadn't carried back low interest rate financing and the first was obtained from an institutional lender at current market terms.

DISCOUNTING THE FACE VALUE OF A LOAN

There will often be a market for a loan—somebody out there will be willing to buy it from a lender (here, a seller who provides financing) for cash. These people constitute the loan purchase market, "make" the rate, and often can be found in the yellow pages and in the financial or classified sections of newspapers. If the loan is purchased at full face value and the same payments are received, the loan purchaser only receives the same rate as the original lender, probably much lower than the loan purchaser requires. The loan payments can't be increased since there is already a contractual agreement. The only way to effectively increase the interest rate is to buy the loan for less than face value. The purchaser (an investor or a loan broker) may purchase a $50,000 owner-carried second for $40,000, thereby increasing the effective interest rate to more than the stated contract rate. In this case, the loan has been sold for a 20 percent discount ($50,000 − 20% = $40,000). The $40,000 is the cash equivalence of the $50,000 favorable financing. If this property is used as a comparable, $10,000 would be subtracted first from sale price since it is considered that the purchaser paid the seller an extra $10,000 to provide the favorable financing. This puts the comparable and subject on equal ground, assuming that the subject is to be offered with typical financing terms (an assumption implicit in the definition of market value). The gross rent multiplier, overall rate, and physical approaches to value can now be abstracted and applied to the subject property.

Caution should be used with this method to ensure that the discount rate used isn't so high that only a small percentage of seller/financiers would consider selling the loan at the discount rate.

ANOTHER METHOD FOR COMPUTING CASH EQUIVALENCE

The quickest way to obtain cash equivalence is to discount the face value of the loan in the manner demonstrated above. An alternative technique, actually favored by many as more indicative of market behavior, is to apply the market *interest rate* to the loan income stream, discounting the income stream to a present value or cash equivalent. To adjust a comparable sale:

1. Determine the payments on the loan to be converted, adding any balloon payment to the final periodic payment.
2. Determine today's market rate of interest for such a loan.
3. Using the market rate, discount the income stream (Calculator Procedure 7 for the periodic payment, Calculator Procedure 4 for any balloon payment) to a present value. This is the loan's cash equivalent.
4. Deduct the cash equivalent from the face value of the loan. The remainder is the additional amount paid by the purchaser to obtain the favorable financing.
5. Deduct the additional amount from the comparable's sale price, thereby bringing the comparable and subject to a cash equivalent basis.

This process is demonstrated in the following example.

EXAMPLE 13.1. Discounting a loan to a cash equivalent

Research uncovers an otherwise excellent comparable sale (case study Comparable No. 2) that was sold with a favorable second loan. Particulars of the transaction are as follows:

Sale price	$3,565,000
Cash down	$356,500
First financing	$2,650,000 new conventional loan.
Second financing	$558,500 (owner-carried second at 8% interest per annum, payable monthly, interest only, all due in five years. Payments are $3,723.33 per month)

Income	$465,000 annual gross income
	$302,250 annual net income
Physical description	68 units
	222 rooms
	51,680 square feet

Q. What is the cash equivalence of the second loan if the market interest rate for similar seconds is 12%?

A. The income stream for the second loan is 59 payments (4 years, 11 months) of $3,723.33 plus a final payment of $562,223.33 (final periodic payment plus the payoff). Using Calculator Procedure 7 to discount the series of 59 payments and Calculator Procedure 4 to discount the final payment to a present value gives us the loan's cash equivalence:

Calculator Procedure	Discount Rate	Amount/Type	Present Value
7	12%/12	$3,723.33 for 59 periods	$165,332.94
4	12%/12	$562,223.33 at 60th period	309,475.62
			$474,809

Cash equivalence of second loan

Q. What is the sale's cash equivalence for comparable purposes?

A. Adjusting the sale price to a cash equivalence for comparable purposes is done in this way:

Face amount of second	$558,500
Cash equivalence	474,809
Price paid for favorable financing	$ 83,691
Sale price	$3,565,000
Price paid for favorable financing	83,691
Cash equivalent sale price	$3,481,309

Q. What is the indicated gross rent multiplier? Overall rate? Dollars per unit? Dollars per room? Dollars per square foot?

A. Units of comparison are based on the cash equivalent price:

Gross rent multiplier $\dfrac{\$3{,}481{,}309}{\$465{,}000} = 7.49$

Overall rate $\dfrac{\$302{,}250}{\$3{,}481{,}309} = 8.68\%$

Dollars per unit $\dfrac{\$3{,}481{,}309}{68} = \$51{,}196$

$$\text{Dollars per room} \quad \frac{\$3{,}481{,}309}{222} = \$15{,}682$$

$$\text{Dollars per square foot} = \frac{\$3{,}481{,}309}{51{,}680} = \$67.36$$

Looking at the problem from a different standpoint, the cash equivalent sale price can also be computed as the cash equivalence of the loan plus the cash downpayment.

cash equivalent sale price = loan cash equivalency + cash downpayment

In Example 13.1 the second question also could have been computed in this way:

Cash equivalence of first	$2,650,000
Cash equivalence of second	474,809
Downpayment	356,500
Cash equivalence of sale	$3,481,309

SELECTING A RATE

The best method for selecting the appropriate interest rate is to go to the market. In the absence of a market rate for a particular type of loan, a rate must be selected based on other rates, although some adjustment is often needed to reflect the considerations behind the particular loan in question. For instance, the rate for an institutional first would not be applied to a subordinated second that is secured by a higher stratum of the property's value. The following factors are to be considered when selecting the proper market interest rate:

1. *Risk.* Loans are subject to several different types of risk:
   a. Risk of default, especially if the loan is a form of secondary financing and is subordinate to the first.
   b. Risk of no resale market for the loan.
   c. Risk of purchasing power loss.
2. *Liquidity.* By making the loan (or buying it from another lender), the purchaser forfeits the right of immediate access to the funds. Only a periodic loan payment will be realized.
3. *Management.* Management considerations of a loan are usually minimal unless persuasive efforts become necessary to make the borrower pay as agreed. Hence there is also some risk as to the amount of management involved.

The loan interest rate is composed of all three of these factors plus a basic return for the use of the money. An often-used benchmark for composing a market rate is an institutional conventional loan rate adjusted for the risk, liquidity, and management considerations. The benchmark loan and the loan under analysis should be secured similarly, that is, real property, real property plus personal property, and so forth.

CHAPTER FOURTEEN

FINANCING

Few buyers pay all cash for an apartment building; most mortgage the property, giving the loan proceeds to the seller in order to make up the difference between the cash downpayment and the total purchase price. Properties are most often financed for 70 percent to 90 percent of the total purchase price. As such, the type and terms of the financing play a major role in property value. In fact, if financing sources were to disappear and properties had to be bought with all cash, values would undoubtedly fall dramatically.

The following list gives the most frequently used methods of financing apartment purchases:

1. A new loan is obtained from a lending institution such as a bank or savings and loan. Or the source of financing might be a mortgage banker who, like the bank or savings and loan might do, quickly sells the loan to the FNMA or FHLMC. In any case, the amount of this financing is typically for about 75 percent of purchase price. This type of financing generally carries interest rates which are considered to reflect the market level.
2. The purchaser takes over the existing mortgage, making a cash downpayment for the remainder of the purchase price. Due to appreciating values and the previous amortization (pay-down) of the loan, this existing financing is typically for a lesser amount than would be obtainable with a new loan. However, this financing avenue often provides the benefits of a lower interest rate and fewer loan origination fees (such as loan points, appraisal fee, title report, etc.).
3. In addition to the above financing sources, the seller may provide additional financing by taking back a second mortgage on the property. In this case,

the institutional lender generally requires that the seller's loan (or any other second loan) be subordinate to the first loan. By being subordinate, the seller has no recourse against the bank's interest in the property in case the buyer defaults on the payments or other loan terms. Due to the added risk with this type of loan, one would expect its interest rate to be somewhat higher than the bank's loan (depending on the buyer's credit, property condition, buyer's equity in the property, etc.). However, in order to make the sale more appetizing, the seller often agrees to carry such loans at interest rates below those that would be required by any other lender. This often inflates the price and, if such a sale is to be used as a comparable in an appraisal, a cash equivalent adjustment should be made (see Chapter 13). While this type of financing once accompanied most sales, it is now less prevalent due to revised income reporting laws under the 1986 Tax Reform Act.

INSTITUTIONAL FINANCING

Loan programs can vary according to the type of institution. In addition, the finance business is dynamic, and programs are continually falling into and out of favor. Institutions making loans on apartments include the following:

1. *Banks.* At least in California, banks are more active in making construction loans than "permanent" loans (for existing properties). A construction loan is short-term and must be paid off within a year of a property's completion.
2. *Savings and Loan Associations and Savings Banks.* These have been the largest source of apartment financing for existing properties.
3. *Life Insurance Companies.* Life companies are generally interested only in the upper niche of the market—very prime properties of over 50 units.
4. *Pension Funds.* Pension funds have appetites similar to life companies.
5. *FNMA and FHLMC.* These two lenders are mostly involved with existing properties of average size and character. They do not make loans directly, but purchase existing or proposed loans from institutional lenders or mortgage bankers.

LOAN TYPES

Popular loan programs for apartments fall under two categories: fixed-rate loans and adjustable-rate loans. Fixed-rate loans have a set interest rate for the term of the loan. Terms typically range from three to ten years.

Adjustable-rate loans have floating interest rates that change with an index. The index an institution chooses will closely follow the cost of its money sources. Popular indexes are six-month treasury bills and the Federal Home Loan Bank's 11th District Cost of Funds (the percentage at which savings and loan associations borrow) Index. At this writing, savings and loans are making mostly adjustable-rate loans, while life companies are making fixed-rate loans. Because of their exposure to interest rate swings, savings and loans typically charge a higher rate for a fixed-rate loan than for the beginning adjustable rate.

DEBT COVERAGE RATIO

Along with considering the borrower's creditworthiness, lending institutions use two determinants in calculating maximum loan amounts: *appraised value* and *debt service coverage*. Debt service refers to the loan payments, and debt service coverage refers to the amount of payments that the property's net income can support. A break-even debt coverage means that the loan payments exactly match the property's net income.

Lenders use a number they call the *debt coverage ratio*. A debt coverage ratio (DCR) requirement of 1.10 means that the property's net income must be at least 110 percent of the loan payments. The higher the DCR, the less risk for the lender. Debt coverage ratios typically range from 1.00 (break-even) to 1.20. Obviously, borrowers shopping for maximum loans look for lenders with lower debt coverage requirements. Savings and loans, which often use debt coverage ratios of between 1.00 and 1.10, have historically been more aggressive than life companies, whose DCRs are typically 1.15 to 1.25. However, the lower interest rates that life companies offer can reduce payments, thereby making their loan amounts more competitive with savings and loans. Some factors considered by lenders in their selection of debt coverage ratios include property condition, tenancy, location, neighborhood occupancy, and the loan's interest rate. Lenders typically apply the DCR to actual income (not market income), and may be more aggressive as the gap between actual and market incomes widens (assuming actual income is below market income).

DETERMINING MAXIMUM LOAN AMOUNT

Regarding loan-to-value, savings and loans usually do not exceed 75 percent of the appraised value or sale price, whichever is lower. Some will go 80 percent loan-to-value on a sale as opposed to 75 percent maximums on a refinance. Net income is divided by the debt coverage ratio and loan constant, in order to determine the maximum loan-to-value under debt service requirements. Here is an example of estimating the maximum loan amount:

EXAMPLE 14.1 Estimating maximum loan amount

An apartment building has recently sold for $1,000,000 and is appraised at $1,000,000. Its annual income is $85,000 and the lender requires a debt service coverage ratio of 1.10. The interest rate is 9.50 percent with amortization based on 30 years (loan constant of 0.1009—see Chapter 11 for an explanation of loan constant). The maximum loan amount is calculated as follows:

Loan-To-Value

Sale price × loan-to-value ratio	= maximum loan
$1,000,000 × 75%	= $750,000

Debt Coverage Ratio

Net income / DCR / loan constant	= maximum loan
$85,000 / 1.10 / .1009	= $765,835

In the DCR example, the net income divided by the DCR results in the amount of net income that can be used for loan payments. This amount (the amount of the loan payments) is then divided by the annual loan constant in determining the loan amount.

The loan amount is often based on the lowest figure. However, lenders are generally more flexible in applying debt coverage requirements than in applying loan-to-value requirements.

Occasionally, loans are offered with "teaser rates" for the first six or 12 months. These are interest rates which are below the regular rate and are used to entice borrowers. Adjustable-rate mortgages often have this feature. For example, assume the current interest rate for an adjustable-rate mortgage is 9.5 percent. The borrower may be offered an 8.5 percent interest rate for six months, after which time the loan is adjusted to the regular rate. Lenders may use either the 9.5 percent or the 8.5 percent rate in determining the maximum loan amount—you'll have to inquire as to which they are using.

The fees charged by the lender will also have a bearing on the interest rate. Lenders will typically charge a loan fee of between one and three points, with each point being equivalent to one percent of the loan amount (e.g., one point on a $1,000,000 loan is $10,000). Lower interest rates are often available if the borrower pays additional points. The lender can do this because the additional fee increases the loan's yield. For example, an additional two-point charge on a 9.5 percent loan with a ten-year term increases the lender's effective interest rate to

10.09 percent (this assumes a 30-year amortization with payment of the balance at the end of the ten-year term). When market interest rates are used in estimating or checking capitalization rates, they shouldn't reflect rates bought down with unusually high up-front fees.

Rates may also vary according to the term of the loan, especially with fixed-rate loans. Always seeking less risk, lenders generally prefer shorter terms due to their being less susceptible to interest rate swings—no lender wants a portfolio of 10 percent loans when rates jump to 12 percent.

Obviously, the maximum loan amount and interest rate will vary according to the type of loan and lender. Which type of loan is applicable? For valuation purposes (i.e., when the band-of-investment technique is used to estimate or analyze the overall capitalization rate), I generally use the loan program which is 1) reflective of market rates, and 2) is most often used by borrowers for the type of property under consideration.

CHAPTER FIFTEEN

WRITING THE REPORT

Almost every appraisal assignment requires a written report. Items should be arranged in logical order, beginning with the purpose of the report and ending with the value conclusion, followed by addenda containing burdensome materials that might otherwise interrupt the flow of the report. It must logically present sufficient information so that the reader, often a skeptical review appraiser who considers the report wrong until proven right, can form his or her own value conclusion. As such, the report must provide supporting evidence, reasoning, and conclusions.

Recent falterings of loans and lending institutions have caused lenders to require more information in appraisal reports, mostly in regard to the current health and future of the local apartment market and the expected competitiveness of the subject. Some people argue that the underlying problem is poor loan underwriting, but appraisers are the most organized and regulated group in the lending business and, consequently, this is where a large part of the responsibility has fallen. Be aware of your client's needs in this respect.

FREQUENTLY ENCOUNTERED PROBLEMS IN APPRAISAL REPORTS

These are among the most frequently encountered problems in appraisal reports:

- There is not enough data to support the value conclusion.
- Data are present, but the appraiser does not present reasoning behind conclusions.
- Too much extraneous information is in the appraisal. Some appraisers will include excessive city or zoning data, only to skimp on the discussion of the multiplier or capitalization rate selection.

- The appraisal report raises an area of concern for the client but then inadequately addresses the problem (e.g., rent comparables show excessive vacancy).
- There is insufficient information regarding the financing of the sale comparables.
- There is inadequate information and support as to the current and future health of the local apartment market.
- There are grammatical and mathematical errors. This includes the use of excessive condensations and abbreviations.

The list goes on, but anyone who regularly avoids the above problems has a good start on earning a reputation as a good appraiser.

FORM APPRAISALS

Recent Federal Home Loan Bank (FHLB) policies have supported use of the FHLMC/FNMA appraisal forms for use by their lenders. Their use is given additional encouragement by the secondary mortgage and mortgage-backed securities markets, both of which purchase loans from FHLB lenders. These markets deal in pools of many loans, and standardization is the key for quick review of not just the appraisal but of other loan documents as well.

There are three appraisal forms for apartments: FHLMC Form 72 / FNMA Form 1025 (two pages), FHLMC Form 71B (four pages), and FHLMC Form 71A / FNMA Form 1050 (eight pages). The lender will generally specify the form to be used. Typically, the 1025 is allowed for up to 12 units, the 71B is allowed for loans up to $750,000, and the 71A must be used for anything larger than $750,000. All forms call for three value approaches, and the amount of research required for the completion of all three forms is theoretically the same. Larger properties are of more consequence to the lender, however, and in practice, appraisers will do a more thorough research job for them. It's common to see independent fee appraisers charging five to ten times more for a larger property with a 71A eight-page appraisal than for a smaller property with a 1025 two-page appraisal.

At one time, lenders wanted appraisers to use narrative reports for larger properties (say over 100 units). Now, however, more lenders are endorsing form reports for these properties, so long as enough separate commentary is included to address areas of concern that the form itself might not adequately cover. After including photos, maps, rent rolls, certifications, and other exhibits, many form reports end up with 30 or more total pages.

The FNMA/FHLMC appraisal forms are a typist's nightmare—small boxes and odd spacing, both horizontally and vertically. Computer software for processing the 71A and 71B forms did not really appear until 1987, more than five years after the introduction of programs for single-family residence forms. This software provides not only the advantage of quick input, but ease of correction as well.

NARRATIVE APPRAISAL REPORTS

Narrative appraisal reports are self-contained documents which are often based on a very loosely standardized format. Beyond the logical outline and adherence to good reporting, narrative reports vary as to content and arrangement. The best background for becoming a good narrative report writer is to read other appraisers' narrative reports and to have a sound background in English composition. The most popular reading on narrative reports is "Communicating the Appraisal: The Narrative Report," by William C. Himstreet (Chicago, Ill., American Institute of Real Estate Appraisers, 1982).

One narrative appraisal report that I reviewed several years ago had 33 pages of information on the city in which the property was located, including the mean temperature for all twelve months, amount of rainfall, number of stoplights, etc. While the final value conclusion was based on the income approach, no discussion as given to the derivation of the capitalization rate—it made its first appearance when divided into the net income to arrive at the value estimate. The city information was obviously a previously-canned section that the appraisal company used to bulk up all of its reports on properties located in that city.

While an extreme example, this is a common malady afflicting many appraisal reports. It's also one of the first, and easiest to observe, signs of a lightweight appraisal.

TRANSMITTAL LETTER

This letter is always included with a narrative report and is often included with a form report, as well (Fig. 15.1). Items typically included in the transmittal letter are as follows:

1. Date of the letter (which is probably different from the date of value)
2. Client's name and address
3. Basic information identifying the subject property (This includes address, number of units, whether proposed or existing, and appraiser's and/or client's file number)
4. Type of value being estimated (e.g., fair market value), and the interest being valued
5. Statement of value conclusion and the date of value

ADDENDA

Appraisers may wish to add some pages to the body of the form report (e.g., providing a page of extra sale comparables and referencing it as "page 6a"). How-

October 29, 1988
Our File No. 8875
MS&L File No. AP54321

Metropolis Savings & Loan Association
567 Grand Avenue
Metropolis, CA 90000

Attention: Mr. John Smith, Chief Appraiser

Subject: Appraisal Report
Existing 50-Unit Apartment Building at 213 S. Willson Ave.
Metropolis, California

In response to your telephone request of October 1, 1988, I have conducted the required investigation, gathered the necessary data, and made certain analyses that have enabled me to form an opinion of the market value of the fee simple interest in the apartment building at 213 W. Willson Avenue in Metropolis, California.

Based on an inspection of the property and the investigation and analyses undertaken, we have formed the opinion that as of October 29, 1988, and subject to the assumptions and limiting conditions set forth on page G in the Addenda to this report, the property has a market value of

THREE MILLION TWO HUNDRED SIXTY-FIVE THOUSAND DOLLARS
$3,265,000

The appraisal report that follows sets forth the identification of the property, the assumptions and limiting conditions, pertinent facts about the area and the subject property, comparable data, the results of the investigation and analyses, and the reasoning leading to the conclusions.

Respectfully submitted,

Alan Z. Appraiser

Figure 15.1 Letter of Transmittal

ever, most of the material provided in addition to the form itself is placed in back of the report in a section known as the "Addenda." These items might include any of the following:

- Cover page and table of contents for the Addenda
- Subject property photographs
- Regional and neighborhood maps (Figs. 15.2 and 15.3)
- Survey, assessor's parcel map (Fig. 15.4), or other drawing of the subject site
- Drawings of the building footprint
- Drawings of typical floorplans
- Rent roll
- Historical expense statements
- Photographs of rent and sale comparables
- Maps of rent and sale comparables (Fig. 15.5)
- Legal description
- Title report
- Summary of zoning code, building code, rent control ordinances, or other items which have a special impact on the subject property
- Receipts and/or itemization of recently completed work
- Itemization of work to which the appraisal is subject
- Qualifications of the appraiser(s)

In addition, certain sections of the currently-used appraisal forms are outdated or inadequate. These sections include definition of value, assumptions and limiting conditions, and the certificate of appraisal. You may wish to strike these sections on the form and reference revised pages in the Addenda. Examples of various Addenda items have been included in other chapters of this book. The following four figures provide examples of how maps might look. Note that each map includes a scale and directional arrow.

STANDARDS FOR APPRAISAL REPORTS

Most appraisal organizations publish certain report writing standards to which their membership must adhere. The standards of the major organization, the Appraisal Foundation, are those which are most often cited and followed. Provided below are the Foundation's Standards Rules 2–1, 2–2, 2–3 and 2–4. These are the minimum standards that anyone should use in preparing an appraisal report.

Figure 15.2. Regional Map

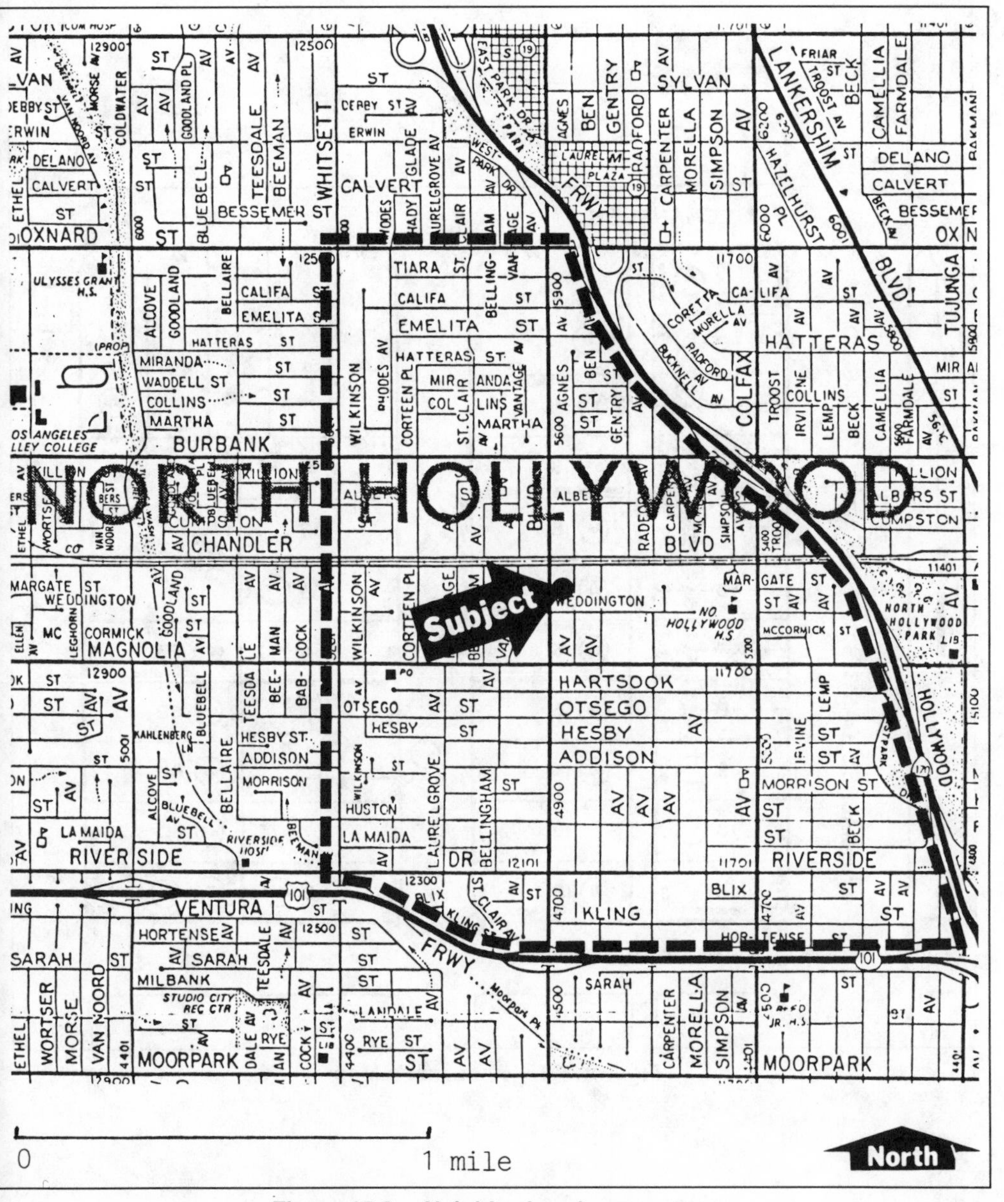

Figure 15.3. Neighborhood map

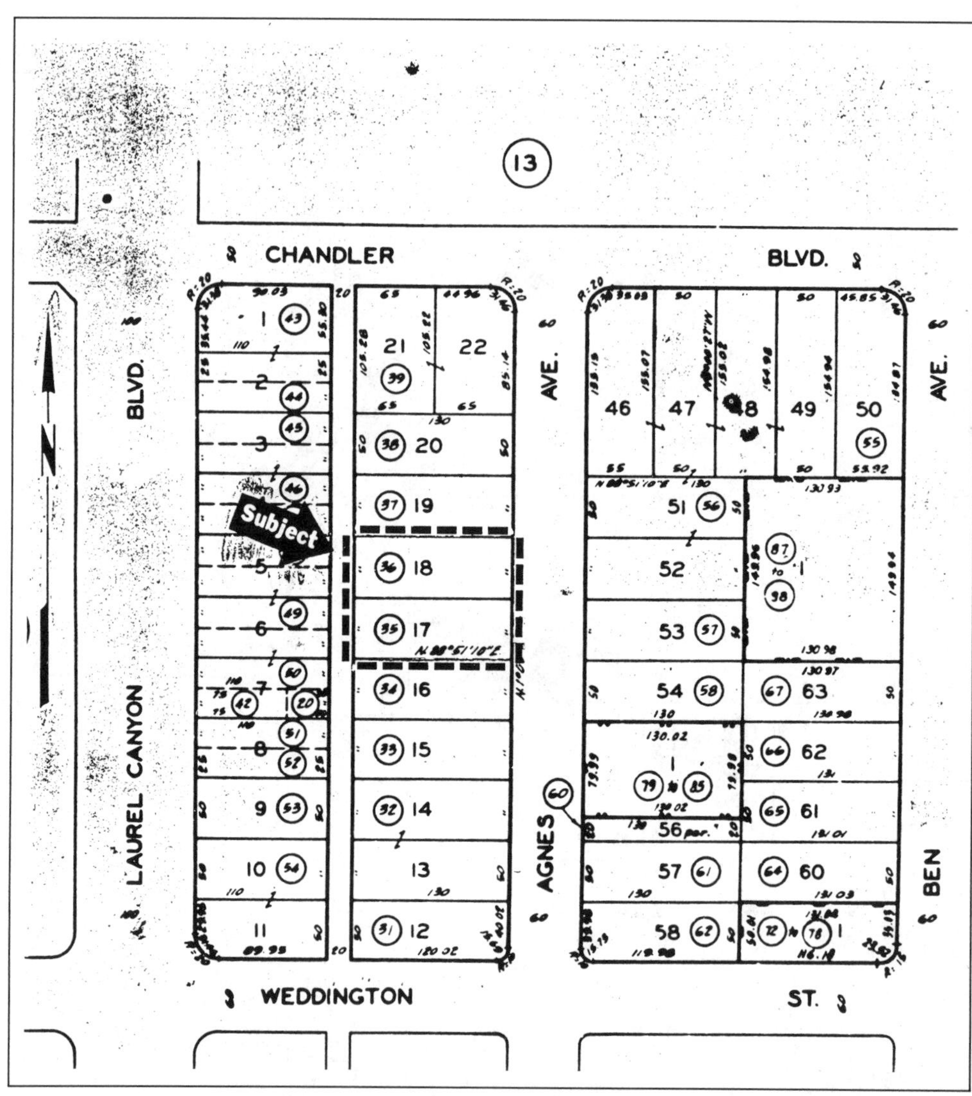

Figure 15.4. Assessor's Map

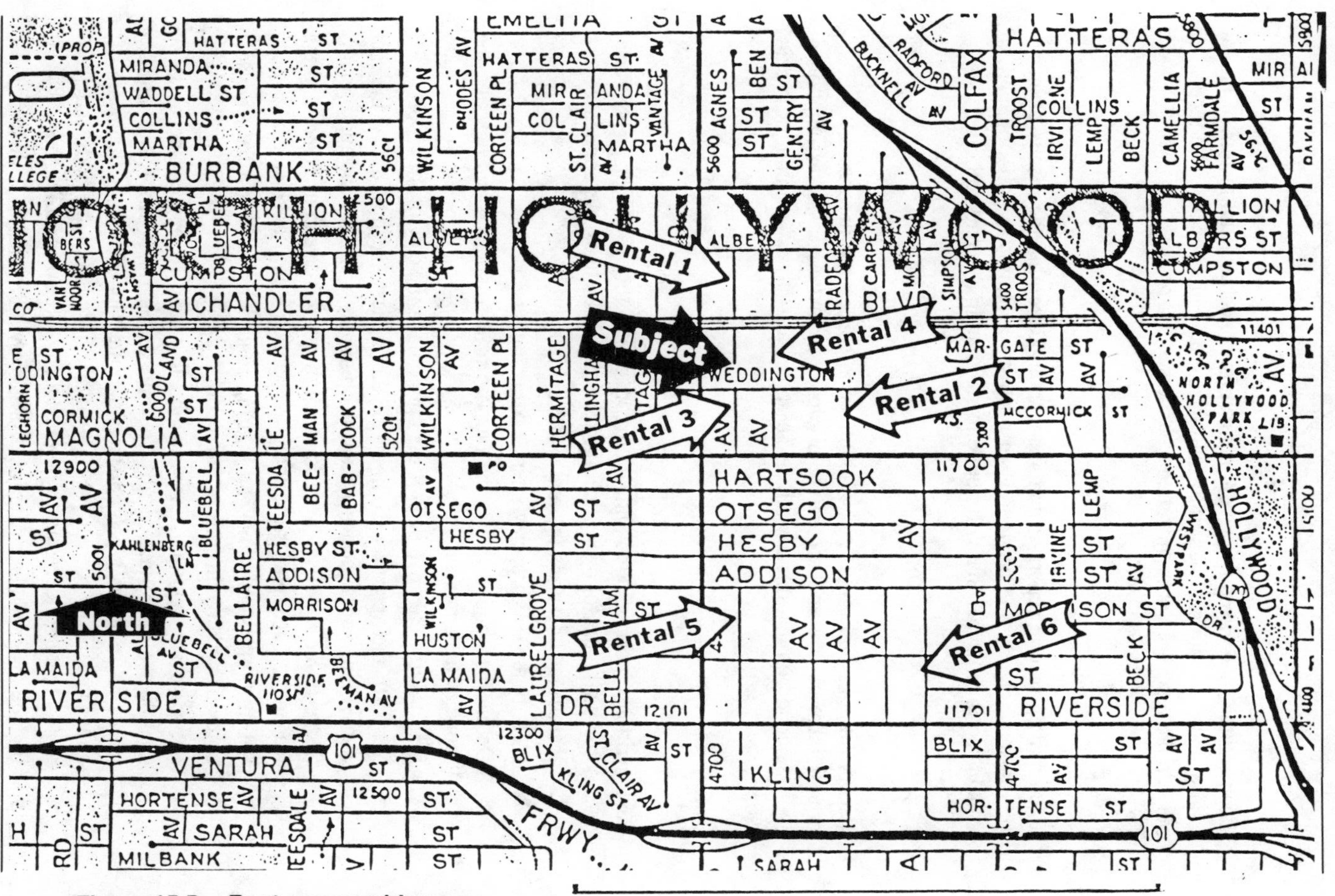

Figure 15.5. Rent comparables map

S.R. 2–1

Each written or oral report or communication concerning the results of an appraisal must contain sufficient information to enable the persons who receive or rely on the report or communication to understand it properly.

S.R. 2–2

Each written or oral report or communication concerning the results of an appraisal must clearly and accurately set forth the appraisal analysis, opinion, or conclusion in a manner that will not be misleading in the marketplace.

S.R. 2–3

Each written or oral report or communication concerning the results of an appraisal must clearly and accurately disclose any extraordinary assumption or limiting condition that directly affects an appraisal analysis, opinion, or conclusion.

S.R. 2–4

Each written report or communication concerning the results of an appraisal must comply with the following specific reporting guidelines. An appraiser must

1. Identify and describe the real estate being appraised;
2. Identify the real property interest being appraised;
3. Define the opinion that is the purpose of the appraisal and describe the scope of the appraisal;
4. Set forth the effective date of the opinion and the date of the report;
5. Set forth the appraiser's opinion of the highest and best use of the real estate being appraised when such an opinion is necessary and appropriate;
6. Set forth the appraisal procedures followed, the date considered, and the reasoning that supports the analyses, opinions, and conclusions;
7. Set forth all assumptions and limiting conditions that affect the analyses, opinions and conclusions in the report;
8. Set forth any additional information that may be appropriate to show compliance with, and identify permitted departures from, the requirements of Standard 1 (which states that the "appraiser must be aware of, understand, and correctly employ those recognized methods and techniques that are necessary to produce a credible appraisal"); and
9. Include a signed certificate in accordance with Standards Rule 2–5.

APPRAISAL GUIDELINES

While the Appraisal Foundation offers requirements for standards and ethics, lending institutions and state and federal regulatory bodies have their own guidelines for how a report should be written and what should be included. Partially based on the guidelines of the various organizations for whom it performs services, Apartment Building Appraisers & Analysts, Inc. has drawn its own guidelines. Appraisal requirements for Fannie Mae's DUS program are provided in Appendix D.

APARTMENT BUILDING APPRAISERS & ANALYSTS, INC.

These guidelines do not address all of the basics of appraising—it goes without saying that our work is to conform to good and accepted appraisal practice. Most of the items presented below are meant as improvements which will benefit our clients' reviewers and underwriters.

I. STANDARDS

All appraisals are to conform with the Standards of Professional Practice of the American Institute of Real Estate Appraisers. In addition, all appraisals done for FHLB-regulated institutions are to conform to FHLB regulations. When available, any appraisal guideline memorandas from the client must also be followed.

II. FORMAT

The Appraisal Assignment Sheet will specify the format (either narrative or a form). A transmittal letter and full Addenda are to be included with either format.

III. DEFINITION OF FAIR MARKET VALUE

Unless otherwise specified, the definition of fair market value is to be that currently published by FHLB. The definition as provided on the front of appraisal Form 71A is to be struck, and reference is to be made to the location in the report where the correct definition appears (generally in the front part of the Addenda).

IV. NEIGHBORHOOD DESCRIPTION

As well as containing all essential elements, special attention should be given to the neighborhood's housing inventory. This includes the mix of SFRs, condominiums and apartments; range and typical condition; rent ranges; and SFR and condominium prices. The stage of the neighborhood's life cycle should be specified (growth, stability, decline, or revitalization), as should any current or anticipated changes in land use. Finally, a statement should be made as to how the subject's marketability (from both a rental and sale standpoint) compares with that typically observed in the neighborhood.

V. SITE DESCRIPTION

All properties must be analyzed for compliance with current density and parking codes. If compliance is deficient, provide information as to what the requirements are. Also, if zoning calls for less density, a statement must be made as to how many units can be rebuilt if a certain amount (please specify) of the property is destroyed.

Inquire as to any recent or upcoming benefit assessments that will create an extra tax burden for the subject. This is especially applicable in developing areas.

VI. IMPROVEMENT DESCRIPTION

At least one of each of the different unit types must be inspected and measured for rentable square footage (excludes area covered by perimeter walls). The Floorplan Sketch must show the location of the walls, identify each room and closet, and show all math calculations. Inspection of top-floor units should be made where there is any suspicion of roof leakage. This is the best opportunity to investigate the quality of management. Be sure to inquire as to the following:

1. Are there any persistent maintenance problems?
2. What services are performed by on-site management (especially in regard to services that might otherwise be performed by an outside contractor, such as pool, landscape, and building maintenance)?
3. What is the typical vacancy and turnover rate?
4. Are there any problem tenants? What is the collection loss factor?
5. Where do the tenants work? What percentage of the tenants have children?
6. What items have been recently replaced? What items will soon need replacement? Are the inspected units representative of the others in the complex?
7. How long has current management been in place?

The above items should all be reported in the appropriate sections of the appraisal.

VII. COST APPROACH

Identify the cost service or other source used in the cost estimate. Obtain actual fees (e.g., school, parks, utilities) when available. Provide terms of sale and assessor's parcel numbers for each land sale comparable. Address each of the different types of depreciation.

VIII. COMPARABLE RENTAL DATA AND ANALYSIS

Provide at least four rent comparables; at least six if the property is proposed or more than 10 percent vacant. Provide at least three comparables for each of the subject's unit types; more comparables for specific unit-types that comprise a large percentage of the complex. It is recommended that in the report, the comparables be ordered from least to most expensive. Be sure to inquire as to the following:

1. Are any rent concessions being offered? If so, the concessions are to be discussed in the report and an estimate of the effective rent is to be made.
2. How many parking spaces are being offered with the unit? How much does any additional parking cost?
3. What type of unit is in most demand?
4. What are the typical vacancy and turnover rates?
5. What are the reasons for ranges in rentals? What is the additional rent commanded by corner and/or view units?

The comparables should bracket the subject in respect to price and overall appeal (some superior, some inferior). Rental figures are to be those actually achieved (not asking rents). Rent comparables should appear in order of price (least to most expensive).

Reasons for any comparable's excessive vacancy must be stated within the report. The overall vacancy factor for the comparables is to be stated (in Form 71A, this should appear on the "General Comments" lines in the "Comparable Rental Data" section). If any of the comparables have excessive vacancies attributable to causes other than general market conditions (e.g., in rent-up phase, recent eviction program), a revised vacancy factor that omits these properties should also be reported.

IX. SUBJECT'S INCOME ESTIMATE

Report actual income regardless of the type of income that will be used in the appraisal process. Make mention of the term of the rental agreements, (e.g., month-to-month, one-year) and whether any rental concessions were made. Specify current asking rents. Inquire as to any income from sources such as storage and parking. If a rent roll is not included in the report, stipulate why there is none.

X. OPERATING EXPENSE ESTIMATION

An operating expense history for the past two years should be obtained for any existing property. If not available, a statement should be made as to why it isn't. Methodology for expense estimation should follow that described in our *Operating Expense Guideline*.

XI. COMPARABLE SALE DATA

At least five sale comparables are to be included. More should be provided if they suffer from poor comparability. The comparables should bracket the subject in terms of overall appeal and price per unit. Three should have closed within the past six months.

Full financing information and, if applicable, cash equivalency calculations are to be provided for at least five of the comparables. If these items are not available, the following statement should be made: "Financing data are not available and reliance on this sale is thus limited."

Current listings which indicate the top of the market are also important. A table of earnings-ratio adjustments for the physical indicators should be included in the report.

Especially for properties over $2 million in value, the comparables' on-site management should be surveyed as to the current rent levels (this information to subsequently appear in the report) and compared to the income at time of sale. The comparables' analysis as well as the appraisal process should properly reflect any unusual income upsides perceived by the investor. Unless otherwise specified, an as-is value must be provided for all properties that are being appraised subject to further improvements.

ALL SALES COMPARABLE INFORMATION MUST BE VERIFIED WITH AT LEAST ONE OF THE PARTIES TO THE TRANSACTION (PRINCIPAL OR BROKER).

XII. RECONCILIATION

Reconciliation statements are to be custom-tailored to your appraisal, and not be reiterations of standard boiler-plate language. Always state your conclusion as to the property's marketability. State whether the property has been sold within the past three years or whether there are any pending sales or listings. Include price and terms.

XIII. ADDENDA

Every appraisal is to have Addenda, which contain any of the following items that are possibly obtainable:

1. Table of Contents
2. Correct definition of fair market value
3. Regional map
4. Neighborhood map
5. Assessor's parcel map
6. Building sketch
7. Floorplan sketch with interior walls
8. Rent roll
9. Maps (with scale and directional arrows) of sale and rent comparables
10. Operating expense history
11. Assumptions and limiting conditions
12. Certificate of Appraisal
13. Qualifications of the appraiser(s)
14. Photographs

Please include any other items pertinent to value or loan underwriting.

XIV. PHOTOGRAPHS

All photographs are to be 35mm color. At lest 15 photos of the subject should be provided and well captioned. The following photographs of the subject are to be supplied:

1. Front view
2. Both sides
3. Rear
4. Roof (if possible)
5. Parking area
6. Typical kitchens and baths
7. Any deferred maintenance reported in the appraisal
8. Street (both directions)
9. Property across from which subject fronts
10. Alley (both directions)
11. Any nearby inharmonious uses
12. Nearby properties which have a substantial impact on the subject

Photos of all rent and sale comparables must be included in the report. These photos should be taken from an angle, so that not only the front is shown but the most revealing side as well. Be aware of the client's requirements for additional sets of photos. All negatives must be retained in the appraisal file.

XV. GENERAL

1. Provide commentary as to any unusual aspects of the subject property.
2. Fully address any potential "red flags" such as excessive vacancy in the comparables, deferred maintenance, or high GIM or $/unit used for the subject.
3. When using Form 71A, use the open box at the bottom of page 1 to summarize the subject property's location, condition, occupancy, management, marketability and any unusual factors.
4. Leave no blank lines when using forms. If no entry is made, note your intentions by using "N/C," "----," "xxxx," or "****."
5. Write the appraisal so that the proverbial reviewer located on the opposite side of the country will need no further information, can correctly visualize the property and understand its market, follow your logic, and be able to make his or her own judgment of the property's market value and marketability.

CHAPTER SIXTEEN

DISCOUNTED CASHFLOW, PRESENT VALUE, AND INTERNAL RATE OF RETURN

Discounted cashflow (DCF) is an additional method of estimating value. It belongs to the income approach family, differing from direct capitalization in that a projection of several years' income (which include the final resale proceeds) is used in the valuation process—not just a single year's income. A "discount rate," which is mathematically the same thing as an interest rate, converts the projected income stream for a projected holding period, usually five to 10 years, into an estimate of present value. DCF can be used to arrive at its own value as well as to test the validity of a previously calculated value estimate (e.g., one estimated through the market approach or direct capitalization).

While the market approach relies heavily on the principle of substitution, DCF is based on the principle of anticipation (value is created by the anticipation of future benefits). In practice, it is rarely used for existing small properties. Depending on the complexity and number of the cashflow projections, a personal computer is usually desirable for performing the numerous calculations. A spreadsheet program such as Lotus is ideal for this sort of work.

Discounted cashflow is often most appropriate for office or retail properties where the annual income figures take on abnormal patterns due to below-market leases, leases with unusual income patterns, leasing commissions, participation leases, and so on. In these situations, a single year's net income may not be representative of the property's anticipated income potential. DCF still works for apartments, and its acceptance as a method of valuation stems largely from its frequent use by institutional investors (hence, its greater applicability to larger properties).

Also, lenders and other appraisal clients sometimes require it as a part of the appraisal.

CASHFLOW PROJECTIONS

The case study's first year's net income estimate is the basis for the projection. Certain assumptions must be made regarding the income projections for future years:

1. What is the length of the *projection period*?
2. At what rate will *rental income* change?
3. At what rate will *miscellaneous income* change?
4. Will *vacancy and collection loss* change?
5. At what rate will *expenses* change?
6. What is the *resale price*?

The assumptions are based upon supply/demand factors and market attitudes and expectations. Depending on the assignment and client's needs, cashflow projections most often include loan payments, and some assumptions have to be made about the loan as well. These assumptions may be based on a specific loan which is being considered for the property, or they may be based on typical financing currently available in the market. In any case, any report which includes this type of analysis must clearly state the assumptions on which the analysis is based, and must show the relevant data used in the analysis.

Investors may use after-tax income projections (versus pre-tax projections) to determine what they'll pay for a certain property. Prior to the 1986 Tax Reform Act, a 15 percent pre-tax return typically equated to about higher after-tax return (reflecting advantages of then-favorable depreciation and capital gains treatment)—depending on the investor's tax bracket, financing, and depreciation. However, Tax Reform narrowed this gap. In any case, the usual definition of fair market value describes a typical buyer. Hence, appraisers most often apply the discount rate to pre-tax cashflow figures.

Use common sense is the only solid rule with regard to making the assumptions upon which to base the cashflow projection. We live in an inflationary economy, and changes in income and expenses are most often assumed to be in an upward direction. Assumptions should be reasonable and consistent.

In most applications, the valuation is based on the sum of loan(s) and the present value of the cashflows to the equity position. Note that the final year's cashflow includes the resale proceeds. In other words, the value equation is: Loan amount plus value of equity position equals value.

EXAMPLES OF CASHFLOW PROJECTION

Figure 16.1, what would be the uppermost portion of the printout, gives the assumptions for the variables in Figure 16.2. The projections are done on a personal computer with a Lotus spreadsheet program. The upper half of Figure 16.2 shows the sequence of the calculations as well as some interesting figures. The lower half of Figure 16.2 provides the value estimates and, for the reviewer's edification, the resulting value indicators. Any further explanatory notes to the cashflow can be provided at the bottom. Tables 16.1 and 16.2 explain some of the critical assumptions and numbers in Figures 16.1 and 16.2.

Figure 16.3 is the DCF portion of the R41Z Apartment Integrated Valuation Model developed by Jim Mason, MAI, and Steve Mason. The projection figures are basically the same as shown in Figure 16.2; the Masons' model is provided here to demonstrate a different report format. The six dollar difference between the two exhibits' present value figures (discount rate of 13 percent) is a result of differences in rounding. The Masons' model, which is used in conjunction with Lotus 1-2-3

```
                     FIVE YEAR CASH FLOW PROJECTION
                     AND PRESENT VALUE CALCULATION

                     Property:  Metropolitan Apartments
                     Address:   213 S. Willson Avenue
                     City:      Metropolis
                     Date:      October 1988

**************** PROJECTION ASSUMPTIONS *******************************************

 (1) -->        DISCOUNT RATES
          10.0% = Low value   (highest rate)
          13.0% = Most Likely
          16.0% = High value  (lowest rate)                                   (4)
                                                                              /
                              (2)                                        ESCALATION
                FINANCING        \                INCOME/EXPENSES            RATES
  $2,400,000  = Amount 1st Loan       $441,900  = Rental Income               4.0%
         360  = Amortization Period     $2,400  = Misc. Income                4.0%
      9.500%  = Interest Rate             4.0%  = Vacancy Rate
  $20,180.51  = Monthly Payment        $22,472  = Utilities                   5.0%
                                       $35,556  = Real Estate Taxes           4.0%
                               (3) --> $89,921  = Other Op. Exp.              4.0%

                PROPERTY                          REVERSION
          50  = Number of Units            9.0% = Overall rate        <-- (5)
      39,585  = Number of Sq.Ft.           5.0% = % Sale Expenses
```

Figure 16.1. Assumptions for cashflow projection

****************** CASH FLOW PROJECTION ***

Year	1	2	3	4	5	6
Rental Income	$441,900	$459,576	$477,959	$497,077	$516,960	$537,639
Misc. Income	2,400	2,496	2,596	2,700	2,808	2,920
Sched. Gross Inc.	444,300	462,072	480,555	499,777	519,768	540,559
Vacancy	(17,772)	(18,483)	(19,222)	(19,991)	(20,791)	(21,622)
Eff. Gross Income	426,528	443,589	461,333	479,786	498,977	518,937
Utilities	22,472	23,596	24,775	26,014	27,315	28,681
Real Estate Taxes	35,556	36,978	38,457	39,996	41,595	43,259
Other Op. Expenses	89,921	93,518	97,259	101,149	105,195	109,403
Total Expenses	147,949	154,092	160,491	167,159	174,105	181,343
Exp. as % S.G.I.	33.3%	33.3%	33.4%	33.4%	33.5%	
Exp. $/Sq.Ft.	$3.74	$3.89	$4.05	$4.22	$4.40	
NET OPERATING INC.	$278,579	$289,497	$300,841	$312,627	$324,872	$337,594
Debt Service 1st	$242,166	$242,166	$242,166	$242,166	$242,166	
BEFORE TAX CF	36,413	47,331	58,675	70,461	82,706	

Reversion

Resale Price	$3,751,044
Resale Expenses	187,552
Balance 1st Loan	2,309,783 ← (6)
Net Reversion	$1,253,709

	1	2	3	4	5	
Annual Cashflow	36,413	47,331	58,675	70,461	1,336,415	← (7)

****************** PERFORMANCE INDICATORS **

	1	2	3	4	5
Debt Coverage Ratio	1.15	1.20	1.24	1.29	1.34

LEVERAGED

	Value	Discount Rate	OAR	GIM	$/Unit	$/Sq.Ft.
	$3,179,356	16.0%	8.76%	7.16	$63,587	$80.32
(8) →	$3,278,524	13.0%	8.50%	7.38	$65,570	$82.82
	$3,394,238	10.0%	8.21%	7.64	$67,885	$85.75

Figure 16.2. Cashflow projection report

(version 2.01), includes several other capabilities—including value discounts for absorption periods anticipated for proposed properties (i.e., value loss resulting from rent loss prior to the property reaching stabilized occupancy). Its development was partially subsidized by a grant from the Southern California Chapter of the American Institute of Real Estate Appraisers. For this reason, as well as the Ma-

5-YEAR DISCOUNTED CASH FLOW: Fiscal Year beg Oct-88

	BASIS	CHANGE	Year 1	Year 2	Year 3	Year 4	Year 5	Year 6
Gross Income		4.0%	444,300	462,072	480,555	499,777	519,768	540,559
Vac./Col. Loss	4.0% PGI		17,772	18,483	19,222	19,991	20,791	21,622
Effective Gross			426,528	443,589	461,333	479,786	498,977	518,937
Other Income		4.0%	0	0	0	0	0	0
Total Receipts			426,528	443,589	461,333	479,786	498,977	518,937
Total Expenses	33.30 % PGI		147,949	154,092	160,491	167,159	174,105	181,343
Net Operating Income			278,579	289,497	300,841	312,627	324,872	337,594
Round to			278,579	289,497	300,841	312,627	324,872	337,594

		1	2	3	4	5	Reversion
NOI / Reversion		278,579	289,497	300,841	312,627	324,872	3,751,044
Cost of Resale							187,552
Debt Service / Balance		242,243	242,243	242,243	242,243	242,243	2,309,293
Cash Flow to Equity		36,336	47,254	58,598	70,384	82,629	1,254,199
Discount Rate @ >>	13.0%	0.8850	0.7831	0.6931	0.6133	0.5428	0.5428
PV of Equity Cash Flows >>>>>>>>		32,156	37,007	40,611	43,168	44,848	680,729

Present Value of Equity		878,518
Mortgage Amount	73.2%	2,400,000
Indicated Property Value		3,278,518
Round to		3,280,000

Figure 16.3. Masons' cashflow projection report

Table 16.1. Important Items in the Figure 16.1 Cashflow Projection Assumptions

Number	Term	Description
1	Discount rate	Selected by appraiser and used to value the income stream. In this case, we are using three different rates (based on most likely, optimistic, and pessimistic expectations).
2	Income	Taken directly from the appraisal.
3	Operating expenses	Separated because of their different escalation rates.
4	Escalation rates	Annual rates at which the income and expense categories are assumed to change.
5	Reversion overall rate	The overall rate used to estimate the resale price at the end of the holding period. Note that this is applied to the *following* year's net income figure (as this is how the buyer would probably figure the purchase price). A conservative approach has resulted in the 9.0% resale overall rate being greater than the 8.5% rate selected for appraisal purposes.

sons' own generosity, the cost of the model and documentation has been kept down to $35.00. It can be ordered by contacting the Masons at 1339 Beaudry Blvd., Glendale, CA 91208.

THE DISCOUNT RATE

Discounted cashflow is not considered as reliable as the other approaches, partly due to the difficulty of selecting a discount rate from comparable sales. Also, few buyers use DCF, so there usually isn't a broad enough base from which to gather information regarding general rate expectations. One of the best sources is large

Table 16.2. Important Items in the Figure 16.2 Cashflow Projection

Number	Term	Description
6	Reversion	Projected resale proceeds that are realized in the final year
7	Cashflow	Those figures that discount rate converts into an estimate of value
8	Value	The resulting value estimates based on the previously specified discount rates

brokerage companies that occasionally survey institutional investors as to their discount rate requirements.

The selected discount rate should reflect buyers' expectations as to a reasonable return on investment. While apartment buildings are a unique type of investment, there are alternative investments that are bought and sold at stipulated returns. These include federal treasury certificates, bank certificates of deposit, municipal bonds, corporate bonds, and mortgage loans. These markets offer investment alternatives at rates of return that are stated up-front. Apartment buildings compete with these investments and must offer a potential return that is competitive. As such, you can comparatively shop rates and select one which you feel is appropriate for the subject property.

RISK, LIQUIDITY, AND MANAGEMENT

When researching rates of return, you should consider the risk, liquidity, and management profile of the competitive investment and how it compares to the property being appraised. Pay special attention to the subject property's overall ownership appeal, as apartments can differ substantially one from another.

Risk

It is inevitable that the actual performance of the investment will vary somewhat from the projections, and a degree of risk is always present when the amount or direction of the variances are not known. The following facts outline the risk that you must consider when selecting a discount rate.

1. Changes in market trends, population trends, demographics, and economics can affect future rent levels and expenses.
2. A building might show an adequate rate of return but might also be especially susceptible to governmental actions such as rent control, condemnation, zones changes, and changes in tax law.
3. Little can be done to thwart exterior nuisances such as neighborhood decline, visual blight, noise, and odors.
4. Excessive costs, due to unforeseen failure of structural and mechanical systems or casualty losses, are not figured into the cashflow projection.
5. A financial risk is undertaken when the investment is heavily leveraged, and loan payments are so high that they jeopardize the ability of the investor to meet payments.

These risks should be considered when selecting the discount rate.

Liquidity

Liquidity is a measure of an investment's ability to be converted into cash. The more liquid the investment, the easier it can be converted into cash in a reasonable period of time without the sacrifice of sale price or terms.

Liquidity is desirable because of occasional and unexpected cash needs, as well as the possibilities of encountering more profitable investment opportunities in the future. Since it, too, is based on uncertainties, it is really another form of risk.

In liquidity, real estate ranks poorly compared to other investments, but should compensate by providing a greater return. A single-family house is usually the most liquid form of real estate because of continued demand and the availability of financing. Apartment buildings (depending mostly on the financing market) often rank second, ahead of office buildings, industrial properties, and raw land. Withdrawing equity dollars from special use properties can be very difficult.

Management

In an optimal situation, with on-site management, the investor has only to sit back and collect a check at the end of the year with no mental or physical exertion at all. Headaches will persist, however, and there probably will be some time requirement, which could range from accounting duties all the way to a complete renovation project or other management-intensive situation requiring a full-time commitment.

MATHEMATICS OF THE DISCOUNT RATE

When investing money in a savings account, one expects some amount of interest and, consequently, a growth of one's money over a period of time. One dollar invested in a compound interest savings account at eight percent results in the following growth:

End of Year		Growth
(Start)		$1.0000
	+	8%
1		$1.0800
	+	8%
2		$1.1664
	+	8%
3		$1.2597

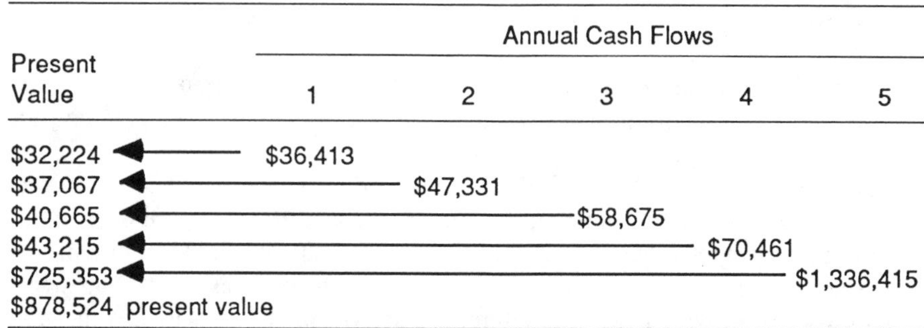

Annual Cash Flows
Present Value
1
2
3
4
5
$32,224
$36,413
$37,067
$47,331
$40,665
$58,675
$43,215
$70,461
$725,353
$1,336,415
$878,524 present value

Figure 16.4. Present value calculation (This format is taken from *Apartment Building Valuation, Finance & Investment Analysis*, John Wiley & Sons, 1982.)

The original dollar has grown to $1.2597 by the end of Year 3. You probably see that as well as being the growth rate, it is also an interest rate. Conversely, what would $1.2597 receivable at the end of Year 3 be worth today if *discounted* back to the present at eight percent per year? The answer: one dollar. In this case, we are using a discount rate of eight percent to find the present value of an amount receivable in the future.

If discounted to the present at six percent, the $1.2597 would be worth $1.0577. Discounted at 10 percent, it would be worth $0.9464. As you can see, the higher the return requirement, the lower today's value of the future receivable.

For DCF appraisal purposes, the selected discount rate is applied to each of the annual cashflows (Calculator Procedure No. 7). If the equity portion of the cashflow projection is that which is being discounted, the loan amount must be added to the present value of the equity in order to estimate property value. Figure 16.4 visually demonstrates the discounting of the all-cash cashflow projection, as shown in Figure 16.2, at the rate of 13 percent.

The present value estimate is $878,524. This represents the value of the cashflows to the investor. This, added to the loan amount, equals the total value estimate of $3,278,524.

The present value figure is close to the reconciled value of $3,265,000 as achieved through our conventional appraisal methods (market and income approaches). In actuality, arriving at a $3,265,000 present value would require a 13.38 percent discount rate.

INTERNAL RATE OF RETURN

The internal rate of return (IRR) on an investment is the discount rate which discounts all of the cashflows back to equate to the initial investment (or in our case,

****************** CASH FLOW PROJECTION **

Year	1	2	3	4	5	6
Rental Income	$441,900	$459,576	$477,959	$497,077	$516,960	$537,639
Misc. Income	2,400	2,496	2,596	2,700	2,808	2,920
Sched. Gross Inc.	444,300	462,072	480,555	499,777	519,768	540,559
Vacancy	(17,772)	(18,483)	(19,222)	(19,991)	(20,791)	(21,622)
Eff. Gross Income	426,528	443,589	461,333	479,786	498,977	518,937
Utilities	22,472	23,596	24,775	26,014	27,315	28,681
Real Estate Taxes	35,556	36,978	38,457	39,996	41,595	43,259
Other Op. Expenses	89,921	93,518	97,259	101,149	105,195	109,403
Total Expenses	147,949	154,092	160,491	167,159	174,105	181,343
Exp. as % G.G.I.	33.3%	33.3%	33.4%	33.4%	33.5%	
Exp. $/Sq.Ft.	$3.74	$3.89	$4.05	$4.22	$4.40	
NET OPERATING INC.	$278,579	$289,497	$300,841	$312,627	$324,872	$337,594
Debt Service 1st	$242,166	$242,166	$242,166	$242,166	$242,166	
Cashflow Before Resale	36,413	47,331	58,675	70,461	82,706	

Reversion		
	Resale Price	$3,751,044
	Resale Expenses	187,552
	Balance 1st Loan	2,309,783
	Net Reversion	$1,253,709

Equity Cashflow					
(865,000)	36,413	47,331	58,675	70,461	1,336,415

****************** PERFORMANCE INDICATORS **

	1	2	3	4	5
Debt Coverage Ratio	1.15	1.20	1.24	1.29	1.34
Equity CF Rate	4.2%	5.5%	6.8%	8.1%	9.6%
100% Equity CF Rate	8.5%	8.9%	9.2%	9.6%	10.0%

Equity IRR	13.38%	Gross Rent Multiplier	7.35
		Overall Rate	8.53%
% Cash Down	26.5%	$/Unit	$65,300
1st Year CF Rate	4.2%	$/Room	$18,343
1st Year DCR	1.15	$/Sq.Ft.	$82.48
		Ave. Rent/Sq.Ft./mo.	$0.930

Figure 16.5. IRR cashflow projection

the appraised value). In our case study, it's noted that 13.38 percent is the rate which discounts the projections back to the $3,265,000 value estimate—this is the internal rate of return.

As such, the IRR is a method of checking a predetermined value estimate (rather than a means of estimating value). Figure 16.5 depicts an IRR cashflow projection model for our case study. The cashflow projections are the same as those shown in the present value model (Figure 16.2). The only real change is that the appraised value is known, and the discount rate (internal rate of return) is unknown. Finally, in using the IRR model to check our $3,265,000 appraised value, we must consider whether the resulting internal rate of return compares reasonably to investors' expectations. If it does, this supports the value as obtained through the conventional appraisal methods. If not, the value estimate should be reviewed.

APPENDIX A

TAX CONSIDERATIONS IN APARTMENT INVESTMENTS

None of the value techniques shown in this book depend on the calculation of tax benefits, despite their being a very important consideration for investors.

The Tax Reform Act of 1986 became effective January 1, 1987, and is currently being phased in over a four-year period. Major tax benefits and considerations, as they will exist under the new law, are as follows:

1. *Depreciation.* Residential rental property placed in service after 1986 is depreciated on a 27.5-year straight-line schedule. Previously, a 19-year accelerated schedule (15 years for low-income housing) was allowed.

2. *Capital Gains.* There is no longer a preferential capital gains tax rate. All capital gains resulting from real property transactions will be taxed as ordinary income.

3. *Passive Losses.* The IRS generally considers rental housing to be a "passive" investment, and disallows losses sustained in its ownership to be used to shelter other income. This restriction is phased in over a four-year period.

An exception is provided: Investors who "actively participate" in an apartment building's management may deduct up to $25,000 in losses per year, providing that the investor's income does not exceed $100,000. This allowance phases out between $100,000 to $150,000 in personal income.

4. *Installment Sales.* Prior to the 1986 Tax Reform Act, installment sales could be structured so that an investor's capital gain could be realized over a period of several years, thereby providing for more advantageous tax planning. The Tax Reform Act has largely ended this advantage.

5. *Rehabilitation Tax Credit.* The tax credit for the rehabilitation of certified historic and some other older structures is lowered from 25 percent to 20 percent.

Use of these credits is phased out for individuals with annual incomes of $200,000 to $250,000.

6. *Construction Costs and Interest.* These costs must now be amortized over the 27.5-year depreciation period.

7. *Tax-Exempt Financing.* Each state has been limited to the amount of tax-exempt bonds which it may issue for housing. Other changes have been made which will narrow the benefit margin between regular and tax-exempt financing.

8. *Tax Rates.* Individual tax rates have been lowered, thereby decreasing the worth of write-offs.

9. *Low-Income Housing.* Some tax credits remain for low-income housing.

10. *Repair and Maintenance Expenditures.* As always, these items can be deducted in the year they are incurred. The rules that distinguish between expenses and capital improvements create a gray area with regard to interpretation. Most owners will opt for immediate deduction (expensing an item) rather than add it to the property basis.

APPENDIX B

CALCULATOR PROCEDURES

Anyone who is serious about appraising income properties must have some mastery of the financial calculator. While several models are available, Hewlett-Packard's 12C has overwhelmingly become the industry standard and is selected for use with the examples provided in this book.

Up until the mid-1970s, every real estate practitioner carried a set of written tables for calculating loan payments, and still required a calculator for factoring in the loan amount. More complicated and time-consuming calculations such as present values, future values, and internal rates of return were considered more as classroom concepts than as useful tools in the real world. The proliferation of the financial calculator has not only made these calculations easier but has also increased the level of sophistication which clients expect in appraisal reports.

The following procedures are designed to get the novice off to a fast start. The Hewlett-Packard manuals are excellent—consult them for more detailed instructions.

CALCULATOR PROCEDURE 1
LOAN PAYMENT*

REQUIRED VARIABLES

1. Loan amount
2. Number of payments
3. Interest rate

Example
A borrower needs a $210,000 loan which is to be amortized over 30 years at 11.75 percent interest per annum with monthly payments. What is the borrower's monthly payment?

HP12-C

Enter		Display	Comments
210000	[PV]	210,000.00	Enters the loan amount
30 [g]	[n]	360.00	Enters the number of monthly payments over the 30-year period
11.75 [g]	[i]	0.98	Enters the periodic interest rate (display answer is rounded)
	[PMT]	−2,119.76	Answer*

*The answer to four decimal places is $2,119.7605. The actual payment will most likely be $2,119.77, since the lender usually rounds up.

NOTE. These examples assume that the decimal place read-out on the calculator is set at two.

CALCULATOR PROCEDURE 2
LOAN BALANCE

REQUIRED VARIABLES

1. Loan payment
2. Number of payments from beginning to end of payment period
3. Interest rate per annum
4. Number of payments per year

Example
A loan was originally made in the amount of $210,000 at 11.75 percent per annum interest amortized over 30 years. Monthly payments are $2,119.77. What is the remaining loan balance after the end of the first year (12 payments)?

HP-12C

Enter		Display	Comments
2119.77	[CHS] [PMT]	−2,119.77	Key in the payment, change it to a negative, and enter it
210000	[PV]	210,000.00	Loan balance at start of calculation
11.75	[g] [i]	0.98	Annual interest rate converted into a periodic interest rate
12	[f] [AMORT]	−24,632.60	Total amount of interest paid during the 12 payments
	[RCL] [PV]	209,195.36	Answer: Remaining loan balance after 12 months is $209,195.36

CALCULATOR PROCEDURE 3
FINDING THE FUTURE VALUE OF A KNOWN PRESENT AMOUNT

REQUIRED VARIABLES

1. Present value
2. Number of growth periods (usually years) from present to future date
3. Growth rate

Example
A cash flow of $11,015 is generated by an investment in Year 1 (assumed to be realized at the end of the year). It is invested to yield 8 percent per annum for the remainder of the five-year period. What will its worth (future value) be at the end of Year 5 (four growth periods)?

HP-12C

Enter		Display	Comments
11015	[CHS] [PV]	−11,015.00	Enters a negative 11,015 as the present value (regarded as a cash *outflow*)
8	[i]	8.00	Enters 8 as the annual growth rate
4	[n]	4.00	Enters 4 as the number of compounding periods
	[FV]	14,985.79	Answer: The $11,015 will grow to $14,986 over four years at an 8 percent growth rate per annum

CALCULATOR PROCEDURE 4
FINDING THE PRESENT VALUE OF A KNOWN FUTURE AMOUNT

REQUIRED VARIABLES

1. Future value
2. Number of periods (usually in years) to the future date
3. Discount rate

Example
A $48,857 renovation project at the end of Year 3 of the holding period is undertaken. The reinvested Year 1 and Year 2 cash flows plus the Year 3 cash flow—totaling $2,486—will be applied to these costs, creating a shortfall of $46,371. What amount must be invested at the start of the holding period to make up the $46,371 shortfall? Assume a 20 percent reinvestment rate.

HP-12C

Enter		Display	Comments
46371	FV	46,371.00	Enters 46,371 as the required future amount
20	i	20.00	Enters 20 as the interest rate at which the amount will be invested
3	n	3.00	Enters 3 as the number of compounding periods
	PV	−26,837.07	Answer: $26,835 invested at 20 percent per annum will equal $46,371 in three years

CALCULATOR PROCEDURE 5
GROWTH RATE

REQUIRED VARIABLES

1. Initial cash outlay
2. Total reversion at the end of the holding period
3. Length of holding period (years)

Example
An initial cash outlay of $93,000 has grown to an amount of $201,622 at the end of the five-year holding period. What is the rate of return?

P-12C

Enter			Display	Comments
201622		ENTER	201,622.00	Enters total reversion
93000		[÷]	2.17	Divides by the initial outlay to find the total growth
5	[f]	[1/x]	0.20	Enters the number of years in the holding period and finds its reciprocal
	[g]	[y×]	1.17	Determines annual growth rate
	[f]	4	1.1674	Displays to four decimal places
	1	[−]	0.1674	Answer: The annual rate of return is 16.74 percent

CALCULATOR PROCEDURE 6
INTERNAL RATE OF RETURN (IRR)

REQUIRED VARIABLES

1. Initial investment
2. Subsequent cash flows

Example
A seller makes a wraparound mortgage. The amount of money funded is $166,150.97. The payments to be received are $2,771.00 for 60 months with the final payment including a balloon payment to the seller of $180,886.53. What is the seller's annual yield (effective interest rate) on the wraparound?

HP-12C

Enter			Display	Comments
166150.97			−166,150.97	Enters the initial outflow as a negative
CHS	g	CFo		
2771	g	CFj	2,771.00	Enters the monthly payment
59	g	nj	59.00	Enters number of payments to be received
183657.53	g	CFj	183,657.53	Enters total of final periodic payment and balloon payment
	f	IRR	1.75	Monthly yield
12	×		21.03	Answer. The sellers's annual yield is 21.03 percent

CALCULATOR PROCEDURE 7
PRESENT VALUE OF A SERIES OF PAYMENTS

REQUIRED VARIABLES

1. Payments and their timing
2. Discount rate

Example
A series of 59 monthly payments of $1,000 are to be received. The annual discount rate for finding the present value equivalent of these payments is 16 percent. What is the present value of the payments?

HP-12C

Enter		Display	Comments
1000	[CHS] [PMT]	−1,000.00	Enters a negative 1,000 as the amount of each monthly payment
59	[n]	59.00	Enters the number of payments
16	[g] [i]	1.33	Enters the annual discount rate converted to a monthly rate
	[PV]	40,670.00	Answer

APPENDIX C

APPRAISAL REPORT

APPRAISAL REPORT
RESIDENTIAL INCOME PROPERTY

TO BE COMPLETED BY LENDER

PROPERTY IDENTIFICATION

File No. ____
Map Reference ____
Census Tract No. ____

Borrower/Client ____
Property Address ____
City ____ County ____ State ____ Zip Code ____
Legal Description ____

Current Sale Price (if applicable) $ ____ Date of Sale ____ Loan Requested $ ____
Terms of Sale ____
Property Rights Appraised ☐ Fee ☐ Leasehold (attach completed Lease Analysis FHLMC/FNMA Form 461)
Lender ____ Lender's Address ____

Instructions to Appraiser: The purpose of this Appraisal is to estimate the current Market Value of the Subject Property. The Definition of Market Value is the highest price in terms of money which a property will bring in a competitive and open market under all conditions requisite to a fair sale, the buyer and seller, each acting prudently, knowledgeably and assuming the price is not affected by undue stimulus. Implicit in this definition is the consummation of a sale as of a specified date and the passing of title from seller to buyer under conditions whereby: (1) buyer and seller are typically motivated; (2) both parties are well informed or well advised, and each acting in what he considers his own best interest; (3) a reasonable time is allowed for exposure in the open market; (4) payment is made in cash or its equivalent; (5) financing, if any, is on terms generally available in the community at the specified date and typical for the property type in its locale; (6) the price represents a normal consideration for the property sold unaffected by special financing amounts and/or terms, services, fees, costs, or credits incurred in the transaction. ("Real Estate Appraisal Terminology," published 1975)

Note: FHLMC/FNMA do not consider the racial composition of a neighborhood to be a relevant factor and it must not be considered in the appraisal.

Other Information: ____
Appraisal Requested From ____ Date ____, 19____ By: ____

ATTACHMENTS

If this Appraisal is made for FHLMC, attach items 1, 2, 5, 6, and 7. Attach additional sheets and check box if considered appropriate for this Appraisal.

1. ☐ Descriptive photographs of subject property
2. ☐ Descriptive photographs of street scene
3. ☐ Photographs of ____
4. ☐ Aerial Photograph
5. ☐ Sketch or floor plan of typical units
6. ☐ Owner's current certified rent roll if existing or, pro forma if proposed or incomplete
7. ☐ Owner's income and expense statement 19____ or pro forma income and expense statement
8. ☐ Map(s) ____
9. ☐ Plot plan or survey
10. ☐ Qualifications of Appraiser
11. ☐ Lease Analysis FHLMC/FNMA Form 461 (required if leasehold interest appraised)
12. ☐ Summary of reciprocal agreements with other owners for use of parking, driveways, recreational facilities, private streets (required if applicable)
13. ☐ ____
14. ☐ ____
15. ☐ ____

SUMMARY OF SALIENT FEATURES

TOTAL NUMBER OF APARTMENT UNITS .... ____
CONSTRUCTION: ☐ Existing Property, Approx. Year Built 19____ ☐ Proposed Construction ☐ Under Construction
DATE OF APPRAISED VALUE .... ____
ESTIMATED MARKET VALUE (Unfurnished) (SEE PAGE 8 FOR CONDITIONS AND REQUIREMENTS) .... $____
Value: Per Unit $____ Per Room $____ Per Sq. Ft. of Building Area $____
GROSS ANNUAL INCOME MULTIPLIER .... ____
OVERALL CAPITALIZATION RATE .... ____%
FORECASTED GROSS ANNUAL ECONOMIC INCOME .... $____
VACANCIES: Actual No. Vacant ____ Percentage of Total Units ____%
Projected Percentage of Forecasted Gross Annual Economic Income ____% .... $____
FORECASTED ANNUAL EXPENSE AND REPLACEMENT RESERVES (____% of Forecasted Gross Annual Economic Income) $____
FORECASTED NET ANNUAL INCOME FROM REAL PROPERTY .... $____
PARKING RATIO .... ____ spaces/units

SUMMARY OF NEIGHBORHOOD AND PROPERTY

NEIGHBORHOOD	GOOD	AVG.	FAIR	POOR
Employment Stability of Immediate Location				
Convenience to Employment Centers				
Protection from Detrimental Conditions				
Adequacy of Shopping Facilities				
Adequacy of Public Transportation				
Adequacy of Utilities				
Police and Fire Protection				
Recreational Facilities				
Property Compatibility				
General Appearance of Properties				
Appeal to Market				

PROPERTY	GOOD	AVG.	FAIR	POOR
Architectural Attractiveness				
Landscaping				
Quality of Construction (Materials & Finish)				
Condition of Exterior				
Condition of Interior				
Room Size and Layout				
Closets and Storage				
Light and Ventilation				
Overal Livability				
Compatibility to Neighborhood				
Overall Appeal and Marketability				

AREA DATA

The ☐ City ☐ County ☐ Area population is approximately ____________

Population: ☐ Increasing ________ % per year ☐ Stable ☐ Decreasing ________ % per year

Describe the economic base which contributes a major influence on the stability of real estate ____________

Discuss employment stability ____________

Rent Control: ☐ Yes ☐ No Comment ____________

Are local Government Agencies discouraging apartment development? ☐ Yes ☐ No Comment ____________

General comments, if applicable ____________

NEIGHBORHOOD AND MARKETING AREA

Type: ☐ Urban ☐ Suburban ☐ Rural Property Values: ☐ Increasing ☐ Stable ☐ Declining

Present Land Use: Built up ______%. Single Family ______% Condominiums ______% Apartments ______% Commercial ______% Industrial ______% ____________ %

Change in Present Land Use: ☐ Not Likely ☐ Likely or ☐ Taking Place From ____________ to ____________

Comment, if applicable ____________

Describe overall property appeal and maintenance level ____________

Describe any incompatible land uses (if none, so state) ____________

Single Family: Price range $________ to $________ Predominant $________ Age ______yrs. to ______yrs. Predominant ______ yrs.

Apartments: Predominant Range in Immediate Area (excluding extremes)

	WALK-UP	ELEVATOR
Number of Units in Each Building	________ Units	________ Units
Age	________ Years	________ Years
Height (number of stories)	________ Stories	________ Stories
Condition	________	________
Rental Range by Unit Type:		
Unit Types: ________	$ ________	$ ________
________	$ ________	$ ________
________	$ ________	$ ________
________	$ ________	$ ________

Comment on any unusual aspects of the above ranges ____________

Est. neighborhood apartment vacancy rate ____%. ☐ Decreasing ☐ Stable ☐ Increasing. Rent Levels are ☐ Increasing ☐ Stable ☐ Decreasing

Describe the unit type(s) by number of bedrooms and rental range that are in the greatest tenant demand ____________

Describe the unit type(s) by number of bedrooms and rental range that are in oversupply ____________

Describe the potential for additional units in area considering land availability, zoning, utilities, etc. ____________

Describe the unsatisfied demand for additional units in area by type and rental ____________

Is population of relevant market area of insufficient size, diversity and financial ability to support subject property and its amenities? ________ If yes, specify.

ITEM	DISTANCE FROM SUBJECT PROPERTY	ACCESS or CONVENIENCE: GOOD	AVG.	FAIR	POOR
Public Transportation					
Employment Centers					
Shopping Facilities					
Grammar Schools					
Freeway Access					

Describe any probable changes in the economic base of neighborhood which would either favorably or adversely affect apartment rentals (e.g. employment centers, zoning) ____________

General comments including either favorable or unfavorable elements not mentioned (e.g. public parks, view, noise, parking congestion) ____________

COST APPROACH

LAND VALUE ESTIMATE: (Include comparable land data if available and appropriate for this appraisal)

ITEM	COMPARABLE NO. 1	COMPARABLE NO. 2	COMPARABLE NO. 3
Address or Location			
Proximity to Subject			
Zoning			
Dimensions or Size			
Shape			
Topography			
Utilities			
Location			
Price			
Sale – Listing – Offer			
Date of Sale			
Price Per Sq. Ft. or Unit			
Comparison to Subject			
Indicated Per Sq. Ft. or Per Unit Value of Subject			

Comments and Reconciliation:

ESTIMATED LAND VALUE: $ ________ per ________ or $ ________

Source of Cost Data: (Optional)

IMPROVEMENTS – ESTIMATED REPRODUCTION COST NEW

________ Sq. Ft. @ $ ________ $ ________
________ Sq. Ft. @ $ ________ $ ________
________ Sq. Ft. @ $ ________ $ ________
________ Sq. Ft. @ $ ________ $ ________
________ Sq. Ft. @ $ ________ $ ________
Carports ________ Sq. Ft. @ $ ________ $ ________
Garage ________ Sq. Ft. @ $ ________ $ ________
Porches, Patios, Balconies, Stairs, Etc. ________ $ ________
Fences, Walls ________ $ ________
Paving, Walks and Lighting ________ $ ________
Landscaping ________ $ ________
Recreational Facilities ________ $ ________
________ $ ________
________ $ ________
________ $ ________
________ $ ________
________ $ ________
________ $ ________
________ $ ________
________ $ ________
________ $ ________
Total Estimated Reproduction Cost New of Improvements ________ $ ________
Less Total Depreciation ________ $ ________
Depreciated Value of the Improvements ________ $ ________
Add Estimated Land Value ________ $ ________
INDICATED VALUE BY THE COST APPROACH (IN FEE SIMPLE) * $ ________
Rounded to .... $ ________

Comments, including explanation of depreciation: ________

* *If property involves leased land, show calculations for fee interest.* ________

Deduct Value of Fee Interest ________ $ ________

INDICATED VALUE OF LEASEHOLD INTEREST BY THE COST APPROACH $

SITE

Dimensions ______ Area ______ Sq. Ft. or Acres

Zoning (classification, uses, and densities permitted) ______

______ Present improvements ☐ do ☐ do not conform to zoning regulations.

Highest and Best Use: ☐ Present use ☐ Other (specify) ______

Site Improvements: ☐ Public Water ☐ Private Well ☐ Public Sewer ☐ Septic Tank ☐ Storm Sewer ☐ Sidewalk
☐ Curbs ☐ Gutters ☐ Alley ☐ Street Lights ☐ Electricity ☐ Gas
☐ Underground Electricity and Telephone ☐ ______

Access By: ☐ Public Street ☐ Private Road Street Surface: ______

Maintained By: ☐ Municipality ☐ Private Association (attach summary of Association documents)

Ingress and Egress (adequacy and safety) ______

Topography, View Amenity, Lot Drainage, Flood Condition, Slopes, etc. ______

Easements or Encroachments On Site and Off Site (if any) ______

Is the property located within a HUD Identified Special Flood Hazard Area? ______

Favorable or unfavorable conditions not mentioned above including any nonconforming use(s) of present improvements. ______

Lot sketch showing lot dimensions, distance to nearest corner, and the location of any nearby detrimental conditions.

(N)

DESCRIPTION OF IMPROVEMENTS

ITEM	DESCRIPTION
Foundation	
Basic Structural System	
Exterior Walls	
Roof Covering	
Interior Walls	
Floor Covering	
Ceiling Heights or Units	Finished Floor to Finished Ceiling is Ft.
Bath Floor and Walls	
Insulation	
Soundproofing	
Heating System, Central or Individual and Fuel	
Air Conditioning System, Central or Individual and Fuel	
Hot Water Heater(s)	
Built-In Kitchen Appliances	
Elevator (No.)	
Plumbing Fixtures	
Security Features	

Construction: ☐ Existing ☐ Proposed Approx. Year Built ______ ☐ Under Construction

Type Project: ☐ Walk-Up ☐ Elevator ☐ Row or Townhouse ☐ Other (Specify) ______

No. of Bldgs. ______ No. of Stories ______ No. of Units ______

Gross Bldg. Area ______ Sq. Ft. Density ______ Units Per Acre

OVERALL IMPROVEMENT RATING	GOOD	AVG.	FAIR	POOR
Architectural Attractiveness				
Quality of Construction				
Condition of Exterior				
Condition of Interior				
Rooms Size and Unit Layout				
Kitchen Facilities				
Closets and Storage				
Soundproofing Adequacy				
Insulation Adequacy				
Electrical Service Adequacy				

Comment on items rated fair or poor and items not covered above. ______

Effective Age Years. Est. Remaining Economic Life Yrs.

PARKING: Total Spaces ______ In Buildings ______ In Garage (separate) ______ In Carport ______ Open (on-site) ______

Parking Ratio ______ Space(s) / Unit. Discuss parking adequacy and convenience to apartment units ______

Driveways, curbing, sidewalks, lighting (adequacy and condition) ______

Describe recreational facilities ______

Describe basement, lobby, garage, laundry, and other building items not described above ______

Comment if any of the above items or other building items are inadequate or are in below average condition ______

Recommended observable repairs: (List repairs, painting, termite treatment, etc. you recommend be made to the improvements to make the property readily marketable; if none, so state). ______

General comments if applicable: ______

COMPARABLE RENTAL DATA

Comparables selected are the most recent rentals, similar and proximate, known to the undersigned, that a tenant of subject property would have given consideration to renting.

ITEM	COMPARABLE NO. 1	COMPARABLE NO. 2	COMPARABLE NO. 3
Address			
Proximity to Subject			
Map Code			
Date of Rental Survey			
Brief Description of Property Improvements	No. Units: No. Vac.: Yr. Blt.:	No. Units: No. Vac.: Yr. Blt.:	No. Units: No. Vac.: Yr. Blt.:
Quality & Condition	Quality Condition	Quality Condition	Quality Condition

Individual Unit Breakdown	Unit Rm. Count			Size	Monthly Rent		Unit Rm. Count			Size	Monthly Rent		Unit Rm. Count			Size	Monthly Rent	
	Tot.	BR	B	Sq. Ft.	$	per sq. ft.	Tot.	BR	B	Sq. Ft.	$	per sq. ft.	Tot.	BR	B	Sq. Ft.	$	per sq. ft.
						¢						¢						¢
						¢						¢						¢
						¢						¢						¢
						¢						¢						¢
						¢						¢						¢
						¢						¢						¢
						¢						¢						¢
						¢						¢						¢

ITEM	COMPARABLE NO. 1	COMPARABLE NO. 2	COMPARABLE NO. 3
Utilities, Furniture and Amenities Included in Rent			
Comparison to Subject			

General comments (including any rental concessions) if applicable: __________

MONTHLY RENT SCHEDULE - SUBJECT PROPERTY

Rental schedule is shown by type of units. Scheduled rents are actual rentals for an existing property, or projected rents for a proposed or incomplete building. Economic rents are forecasted rents to indicate the fair market rental the subject units would command if available for rent on the open market.

No. of Units	Unit Rm. Count			Total Rooms	Sq. Ft. Area Per Unit	No. Units Vacant	SCHEDULED RENTS			ECONOMIC RENTS				
							Per Unit		Total Rents	Per Unit		Total Rents	Per Sq. Ft. or Room	
	Tot.	BR	B				Unfurnished	Furnished		Unfurnished	Furnished			
							$	$	$	$	$	$	¢	$
	◄ TOTAL ►								$			$		

OTHER MONTHLY INCOME

Parking	$ ______	$ ______
Laundry Income	$ ______	$ ______
Commercial Space	$ ______	$ ______
______	$ ______	$ ______
______	$ ______	$ ______
Total Gross Monthly Income	$ ______	$ ______
Total Gross Annual Income	$ ______	$ ______

Utilities Included in Scheduled (actual) Rents: ☐ Water ☐ Gas ☐ Heat ☐ Electric ☐ Air Conditioning ☐ ______

Utilities Included in Economic Rents: ☐ Water ☐ Gas ☐ Heat ☐ Electric ☐ Air Conditioning ☐ ______

If proposed project or project under construction, the rent up time necessary, after completion, to lease 80% of the units at the projected economic rents is estimated to be ______ months.

Comments (including any rental concessions in scheduled rents, or anticipated in economic rents; if none, so state). __________

MARKET APPROACH

The market data selected are the most recent sales of properties, similar and proximate to subject, known to the appraiser, that a buyer of subject property would have given consideration to purchasing. In the absence of actual sales, listings of comparable properties may be used but an explanation must be included in the "Comments" section below.

ITEM	SUBJECT	COMPARABLE NO. 1	COMPARABLE NO. 2	COMPARABLE NO. 3
Address				
Proximity to Subject				
Map Code				
Lot Size				
Brief Description of Building Improvements	No. Units: ____ No. Vac.: ____ Year Built: 19	No. Units: ____ No. Vac.: ____ Year Built: 19	No. Units: ____ No. Vac.: ____ Year Built: 19	No. Units: ____ No. Vac.: ____ Year Built: 19
Quality				
Condition				
Recreational Facilities				
Pool				
Parking				
Tenant Appeal				
Unit Breakdown	No. of Units / UNIT ROOM COUNT: Total, BR, Bath	No. of Units / UNIT ROOM COUNT: Total, BR, Bath	No. of Units / UNIT ROOM COUNT: Total, BR, Bath	No. of Units / UNIT ROOM COUNT: Total, BR, Bath
Utilities Paid by Owner				
Data Source				
Price	$ ☐ Unf. ☐ F	$ ☐ Unf. ☐ F	$ ☐ Unf. ☐ F	$ ☐ Unf. ☐ F
Sale - Listing - Offer				
Date of Sale				
Terms (Including conditions of sale and financing terms)				

Complete as many of the following as possible using data effective at time of sale

ITEM	SUBJECT	COMPARABLE NO. 1	COMPARABLE NO. 2	COMPARABLE NO. 3
Gross Annual Income	$	$	$	$
Gross Ann. Inc. Mult. (1)				
Net Annual Income	$	$	$	$
Expense Percentage (2)	%	%	%	%
Overall Cap. Rate (3)	%	%	%	%
Price Per Unit	$	$	$	$
Price Per Room	$	$	$	$
Price Gross Bldg. Area	$ /sq. ft. bldg. area	$ /sq. ft. bldg. area	$ /sq. ft. bldg. area	$ /sq. ft. bldg. area
COMMENTS				
COMPARISON TO SUBJECT				

VALUE INDICATORS FOR THE SUBJECT PROPERTY

Indicated Gross Income Multiplier ____________ X Gross Annual Economic Income $ ____________ $ ____________

Indicated Value Per Unit $ ____________ X ____________ Units .... $ ____________

Indicated Value Per Room $ ____________ X ____________ Rooms .... $ ____________

Indicated Value Per Sq. Ft. of Gross Bldg. Area $ ____________ X ____________ Sq. Ft. Bldg. Area .... $ ____________

Indicated Overall Capitalization Rate ____________ %

(1) Sale Price ÷ Gross Annual Income (2) Total Annual Expenses ÷ Total Gross Annual Income (3) Net Annual Income ÷ Price

RECONCILIATION: ____________

INDICATED VALUE BY MARKET APPROACH .... $

Rounded to .... $

FHLMC Form 71A Rev. 8/77 Page 6 of 8 FNMA Form 1050 12/83

ANNUAL EXPENSE ANALYSIS

ITEM	☐ ACTUAL 19 ☐ PROPOSED	APPRAISER'S FORECAST	APPRAISER'S CALCULATIONS OR COMMENTS
FIXED EXPENSES:			
1. Real Estate Taxes	$	$	☐ Actual ☐ Est. Total Assessed Value $ % of Value Tax Rate Per $100 $
2. Other Taxes or Assessments			
3. Insurance			
4. Licenses			
5. Unsubordinated Ground Rent			
OPERATIONAL EXPENSES:			
6. Fuel	$	$	
7. Gas			
8. Electricity			
9. Water & Sewer			
10. Trash Removal			
11. Pest Control			
12. Building Maintenance & Repairs			
13. Interior & Exterior Decorating			
14. Cleaning Expenses			
15. Supplies			
16. Elevator Maintenance			
17. Pool Maintenance			
18. Parking Area Maint. & Snow Removal			
19. Gardening			
20. Nonresident Management			
21. Resident Manager's Salary (No. ____)			
22. Resident Manager's Apt. Allowance			
23. Custodian's Salary (No. ____)			
24. Custodian's Apt. Allowance			
25. Engineer's Salary (No. ____)			
26. Elevator Operator's Salary (No. ____)			
27. Telephone Operator's Salary (No. ____)			
28. Security Personnel's Salary (No. ____)			
29. Other Salaries (No. ____)			
30. Payroll Taxes			
31. Advertising			
32. Telephone			
33. Legal & Audit			
34. Leased Furniture			
35.			
36.			
REPLACEMENT RESERVES:			
37. Carpeting & Drapes	$	$	
38. Ranges & Refrigerators			
39. Dishwashers & Disposals			
40. Individual Heating & AC Units			
41.			
42.			
TOTAL EXPENSES & REPLACEMENT RESERVES	$	$	

Comments (identify items by number): ____________________

INCOME APPROACH

Total Gross Annual Economic Income (See Rent Schedule) .... $ ____

Less Forecasted Vacancy and Collection Loss .... (____ %) $(____)

Effective Gross Annual Income .... $ ____

Less Forecasted Annual Expenses and Replacement Reserves (____ % of Total Gross Annual Economic Income) .... $(____)

Net Annual Income from Total Property .... $ ____

Less Return on and Recapture of Depreciated Value of Furnishings ($ ____ @ ____ %) .... $(____)

Net Annual Income from Real Property .... $ ____

Detail clearly method and mathematics of capitalizing Net Annual Income from Real Property ____________________

INDICATED VALUE BY INCOME APPROACH .... $ ____

Rounded to .... $ ____

RECONCILIATION AND VALUE CONCLUSION

Indicated Value by the Cost Approach .... $________

Indicated Value by the Market Approach .... $________

Indicated Value by the Income Approach .... $________

FINAL RECONCILIATION ________

CONDITIONS AND REQUIREMENTS OF APPRAISAL (include required repairs, replacements, painting, termite inspections, etc.) ________

VALUATION: This Appraisal is based upon the definition of Market Value, the Certification, the Contingent and Limiting Conditions, and the requirements that are stated in this report.

As a result of my investigation and analysis, my estimate of Market Value of the subject property as of ________, 19____ is ......

$

Date ________ Appraiser ________

If Applicable, complete the following

Date ________ Appraiser ________

Date ________ ☐ Supervising or ☐ Review Appraiser ________

☐ Did ☐ Did not physically inspect property.

CERTIFICATION: The Appraiser certifies and agrees that

1. The Appraiser has no present or comtemplated future interest in the property appraised and neither the employment to make this Appraisal, nor the compensation for it, is contingent upon the appraised value of the property.
2. The Appraiser has no personal interest in or bias with respect to the subject matter of the appraisal report or the participants to the sale. The "Estimate of Market Value" in the appraisal report is not based in whole or in part upon the race, color, or national origin of the prospective owners or occupants of the property appraised, or upon the race, color or national origin of the present owners or occupants of the properties in the vicinity of the property appraised.
3. The Appraiser has personally inspected the property, both inside and out, and has made an exterior inspection of all comparable sales listed herein. To the best of the Appraiser's knowledge and belief, all statements and information in this report are true and correct, and the Appraiser has not knowingly withheld any significant information.
4. All contingent and limiting conditions are contained herein (imposed by the terms of the assignment or by the undersigned affecting the analyses, opinions, and conclusions contained in this report).
5. This Appraisal Report has been made in conformity with and is subject to the requirements of the Code of Professional Ethics and Standards of Professional Conduct of the appraisal organizations with which the Appraiser is affiliated.
6. All conclusions and opinions concerning the real estate that are set forth in the Appraisal Report were prepared by the Appraiser whose signature appears above on this Appraisal Report, unless indicated as "Review Appraiser." No changes of any item of the Appraisal Report shall be made by anyone other than the Appraiser, and the Appraiser shall have no responsibility for any such unauthorized change.

CONTINGENT AND LIMITING CONDITIONS: The certification of the Appraiser appearing in this Appraisal Report is subject to the following conditions and to such other specific and limiting conditions as are set forth by the Appraiser in the report.

1. The Appraiser assumes no responsibility for matters of a legal nature affecting the property appraised or the title thereto, nor does the Appraiser render any opinion as to the title, which is assumed to be good and marketable. The property is appraised as though under responsible ownership.
2. Any sketch in this report may show approximate dimensions and is included to assist the reader in visualizing the property. The Appraiser has made no survey of the property.
3. The Appraiser is not required to give testimony or appear in court because of having made this Appraisal with reference to the property in question, unless arrangements have been previously made therefor.
4. The distribution of the total valuation in this report between land and improvements applies only under the existing program of utilization. The separate valuations for land and building must not be used in conjunction with any other Appraisal and are invalid if so used.
5. The Appraiser assumes that there are no hidden or unapparent conditions of the property, subsoil, or structures which would render it more or less valuable. The Appraiser assumes no responsibility for such conditions or for engineering which might be required to discover such factors.
6. Information, estimates, and opinions furnished to the Appraiser, and contained in this report, were obtained from sources considered reliable and believed to be true and correct. However, no responsibility for accuracy of such items furnished the Appraiser can be assumed by the Appraiser.
7. Disclosure of the contents of this Appraisal Report is governed by the By-laws and Regulations of the professional appraiser organizations with which the Appraiser is affiliated.
8. Neither all nor any part of the contents of this report, or copy thereof (including conclusions as to property value, the identity of the Appraiser, professional designations, reference to any professional appraisal organizations, or the firm with which the Appraiser is connected) shall be used for any purposes by anyone but the client shown on Page 1 of this report, the mortgagee or its successors and assigns, mortgage insurers, consultants, professional appraisal organizations, any state or federally approved financial institution, any department agency, or instrumentality of the United States or of any State or of the District of Columbia, without the previous written consent of the Appraiser; nor shall it be conveyed by anyone to the public through advertising, public relations, news, sales, or other media, without the written consent and approval of the Appraiser.
9. On all Appraisals involving proposed construction, the Appraisal Report and value conclusion are contingent upon completion of the proposed improvements in accordance with the plans and specifications prepared by ________ ________ with a last revision date of ________ which have been initialed and dated by the Appraiser.

APPENDIX D

FANNIE MAE APPRAISAL REQUIREMENTS FOR ITS DELEGATED UNDERWRITING AND SERVICING PROGRAM

This appendix provides Fannie Mae's (FNMA) apartment appraisal requirements for its Delegated Underwriting and Servicing program, updated as of December 1988. Fannie Mae probably uses more apartment appraisals than any other entity, and the chances are good that some of your work will end up there.

While the previous parts of this book discuss mostly appraisal technique, these requirements address appraisal considerations and good report writing. Once again, note that some of your appraisals will probably end up being reviewed by people located in another part of the country—maybe they've never even been in the city where the subject property is located. These requirements are geared to helping them confidently understand the local economy, apartment market, the property itself, and how well it competes.

APPRAISAL

The following chapter describes Fannie Mae's requirements for valuing multifamily properties under Delegated Underwriting and Servicing. The provisions of this Chapter are based on Fannie Mae's minimum acceptable appraisal standards under Delegated Underwriting and Servicing. This Chapter is intended to identify for the Lender's underwriters and appraisers the information they need to make a prudent underwriting decision. The appraiser's role in this process is to provide an estimate of the market value of the property and a complete, accurate description of the property. All conclusions reached must represent the appraiser's professional conclusion, and must be based upon and supported by market data, logical analysis, and sound judgment.

Fannie Mae recognizes that it may not be possible to apply our guidelines to every appraisal. Therefore, we allow the appraiser discretion in developing the estimate of value. The appraiser must, however, provide sound reasoning for working outside our standards. Any deviations from these appraisal procedures are exceptions and must be appropriately documented and be consistent with normally accepted professional standards and techniques of the appraisal industry. Fannie Mae strongly encourages appraisers to adhere to applicable standards and conduct as established by professional appraisal organizations.

Care should be taken to instruct the appraiser as to Fannie Mae's anti-redlining policy as set forth in Section 301 of this Part, and supplemented in Sections 503 and 508.04 of this Part.

Section 501. Appraiser Qualifications.

Fannie Mae does not approve specific appraisers for purposes of Delegated Underwriting and Servicing. Lenders are responsible for the selection of appraisers and will be solely accountable for their performance.

Fannie Mae expects Lenders to take appropriate steps to ensure that selected appraisers are qualified to appraise multifamily properties. Lenders should review the appraiser's education, multifamily appraisal experience, sample appraisal and professional affiliations. Appraisers must have at least 4 years of income property appraisal experience. Professional appraisal designations from nationally recognized organizations which have formal experience, education and ethics requirements are not required, but can help the Lender in evaluating an appraiser's qualifications. Fannie Mae encourages Lenders to select appraisers from within the market area of the property. If Lenders employ in-house appraisers, they must possess the same professional qualifications and experience as independent fee appraisers.

Fannie Mae reserves the right to notify the Lender at any time that Fannie Mae will no longer accept appraisals made by a certain appraiser.

Section 502. General Guidelines for the Appraisal Report

The appraisal report must be completed using Fannie Mae Form 1050. A narrative attachment to the report may also be necessary. Fannie Mae requires the appraiser and underwriter to meet the requirements described in this Chapter when fulfilling their respective functions in the underwriting process. If, however, the appraiser becomes aware of other items, issues or facts about the property that are not specifically covered by this Delegated Underwriting and Servicing Guide, but which, in the appraiser's opinion, would be important to the Lender or Fannie Mae, the appraiser should report such items in an attachment to the report. The appraisal report must be complete and its conclusions fully documented. The Lender shall promptly return an incomplete report or one lacking credibility to the appraiser with a letter identifying deficiencies.

Section 503. Unacceptable Appraisal Procedures

Fannie Mae categorizes certain appraisal procedures as unacceptable for use in underwriting loans under Delegated Underwriting and Servicing. These are examples of practices which would be considered unacceptable:

- Use of inaccurate factual data about the neighborhood of the property site or about improvements to the property.
- Development of a valuation conclusion that is based—either partially or completely—on the race, color, or national origin of either the Borrower or prospective occupants of the subject property or of the present owners or occupants of the properties in the vicinity of the subject property.
- Failure to comment on any negative factors about the property's neighborhood, or the property's proximity to any adverse natural or man-made influence.
- Selection and use of inappropriate comparables or failure to use comparables that most resemble the property in terms of market area, location and physical similarity.
- Adjustments to comparables that do not reflect the market reaction to the differences between the property and the properties it is being compared to, or failure to make adjustments in comparables when they are clearly indicated.
- Inconsistency of analysis from one indication of value to another that is not reconciled or explained.
- Use of a capitalization rate inconsistent with current investor requirements.
- Unacceptable forecasting of rents.
- Unrealistic expense analysis that is inconsistent with current project expenses, comparable properties, and future trends in the market area.
- Failure to report and analyze any sales transactions, option agreements, or contracts of sale involving the property that are currently being negotiated or that were concluded within the last three years. This requirement includes those transactions or agreements of which the appraiser had or reasonably should have had knowledge.

Section 504. Date of Valuation

The appraisal is for the Lender and must normally be paid for and initiated by the Lender. The date of valuation should not be more than 3 months prior to the date of loan application.

Exceptions to these criteria will be limited to the following:

1. The lender may accept an appraisal presented by the Borrower if the appraisal is completed on Form 1050, the appraiser certifies that the appraisal conforms to the DUS guidelines of this Chapter and the Lender certifies to the content and value conclusion presented by the appraiser.
2. The Lender may accept an appraisal more than 3 months but less than 1 year old if the appraisal conforms to all DUS appraisal requirements, and the original appraiser submits a "change letter" stating that an update of information along with a re-inspection of the property indicates the property's value has not changed appreciably.

Section 505. Documents Provided by the Lender to the Appraiser

The Lender must furnish the following documents to the appraiser:

- Fannie Mae Form 1050 and the information required and definitions used in this Guide. In particular, the Lender must instruct the appraiser to use the definition of "market value" contained in Form 1050.
- Final plans and specifications for a recently completed property, or any work write-ups for existing property, or engineering reports specifically analyzing the feasibility of moderate rehabilitation property and estimating required construction time and the total cost of the planned rehabilitation.
- Owner's certified current rent roll (Form 4243) and, if the property is recently completed or to be moderately rehabilitated, a pro forma statement.
- Owner's income and expense statements for the preceding three years, if available.
- Soil test report, if the property is recently completed new construction.
- As-built survey of the property showing the location of any improvements, and of parking areas, driveways, recreational facilities, setback requirements, easements, lot line dimensions and any special hazard area boundaries. If the property is recently completed, a site plan showing these items.
- Legal description
- Certificate of building bode compliance, or, if the property is to be moderately rehabilitated, the results of a recent codes inspection.

- Copies of any leases for commercial rental space on the property.
- Copies of any ground leases.
- Copies of any reciprocal use agreements relating to recreational facilities, parking areas, private streets, etc.
- Aerial photograph of the property.
- Evidence that the property is serviced by public utilities.

Section 506. Market Study

Fannie Mae requires a market study as part of an appraisal of a property that is recently completed, if sustaining occupancy has not been reached, or of a property that is to be moderately rehabilitated. The study may be a separate report or may be incorporated within the appraisal report. Fannie Mae requires the market study to cover, at a minimum, the following issues:

- Comments on historic, current, and forecasted absorption rates and occupancy levels.
- Cash flow analysis for the rent-up period until the property's income reaches the breakeven point, indicating any operating deficit escrow required.
- Status, extent and impact of present competition in the market, including any properties under construction, properties for which permits have been issued, and properties otherwise known to be in the proposal or planning stage in the market area or beyond the basic market area if they are likely to impact the subject property.
- Population trends and projections.
- Employment levels and trends.

Section 507. Special Requirements For A Moderate Rehabilitation Valuation

For properties to be moderately rehabilitated, Fannie Mae requires an appraisal of the property's value based both on "as is" value and value "as completed."

Section 508. Preparing a Form 1050 Appraisal Report

Form 1050 contains detailed instructions for its completion. This Section provides additional guidelines for preparing this Report.

Section 508.01. Property Identification

The Lender should complete the entry for "Property identification," noting the following items:

- Legal Description—The appraiser must verify the legal description provided. If an attachment is used to furnish the legal description, indicate this on the form.
- Current Sales Price—If the property was sold within the past three years state the sales price. The sales price can be obtained either from a current sales contract or from a recorded deed. Indicate the transaction date and any special terms relating to financing, including loan fees, repairs, remodeling and unusual conditions that should be considered in Market Data Analysis.
- Property Rights Appraised—If the type of interest in which property rights are held is leasehold, it shold be noted that the appraiser must attach a Ground Lease Analysis (Fannie Mae Form No. 461) to the appraisal report.
- Instructions to Appraiser—The Lender should direct the appraiser to the property site and indicate how the appraiser can enter the property for inspection purposes.

Section 508.02. Purpose of Appraisal

The purpose of the appraisal is to establish the market value of the property. This purpose is stated and defined in Form 1050.

Section 508.03. Attachments

The appraiser must attach the following supporting documentation and additional information to the appraisal report:

- A copy of all of the documents supplied by the Lender. The appraiser should consider all of the information supplied in developing the appraisal. The appraiser should comment on any deviations from the pro formas or expense items supplied that were used in the income approach to value. The appraiser must also review and comment on the effect of the commercial lease terms on the value of the property.
- One set of quality color photographs of the property is required. The photographs should be identified with the property's address and the date the photographs were taken. Photographs should be taken of the property (front, side and rear views, and existing improvements), neighborhood and street scenes (including partial view of the property), and comparable rental projects in the neighborhood (even if not reported as comparables). An aerial photograph of the property and the neighborhood should be included.
- Map showing the location of the property and all rental and sales comparables used in the appraisal report. The appraiser will indicate the location of the property and the comparables on the map by means of a key or arrows.

- If the property is held in a leasehold estate, the appraiser should comment on the effect of this type of ownership interest on the value of the property. The appraiser should disclose all calculations used in this analysis by means of an attachment to the report. In addition, the appraiser must complete the required Ground Lease Analysis (Form 461), which is to be attached to the report along with copies of the ground lease and any modifications to the ground lease.
- A statement of the appraiser's qualifications, including education (professional and otherwise), employment experience, principal clients served and major types of properties appraised.

Section 508.04 Summary of Neighborhood and Property

The Summary of Neighborhood and Property required by Form 1050 should be based on the appraiser's careful analysis of the information on pages 2 and 3 of Form 1050. For each property or location characteristic the appraiser should make one of the following ratings based on the standards described below:

Good	If the characteristic is demonstrably superior to other competing properties.
Average	If the characteristic is typical and accords with the norm.
Fair	If the characteristic falls below the norm for competing properties of this type.
Poor	If the characteristic is demonstrably inferior to, and far below, that of competing properties.

A neighborhood analysis should consider the influence of economic, government, and environmental forces on property values in the subject neighborhood. However, neither the racial composition nor the age of a neighborhood is a reliable appraisal factor. A property located in an older neighborhood can be as sound an investment as a property located in a new neighborhood, and a property located in a neighborhood inhabited primarily by members of one race can be as sound an investment as one located in a racially mixed neighborhood. The appraiser must be impartial and specific in describing favorable or unfavorable factors in a neighborhood, and should avoid the use of subjective terms or phrases such as "pride of ownership", etc.

Section 508.05. Area Data

The appraiser should consider the following relevant supply and demand factors, among others, in analyzing the market area of the property:

- Population characteristics of typical tenants in the market area, including family size, occupations and level of education.
- Average family income and the current cost of living factor for the market area.
- Consumer expenditures and total sales in the market area.
- Real estate activity in the market area, including number and dollar volume of sales, as well as availability of financing.
- Vacancy rates for the market area, taking into account various sizes and types of units.

If the property is under rent control, the appraiser should include as an exhibit to their report a *synopsis* of the applicable rent control laws or regulations. The actual rent control laws should be available for review either in the underwriting file or in the appraisers working file. The appraiser should also discuss the community attitude toward rent control and any existing or anticipated rent control laws or regulations. The appraiser should also consider the degree of organized consumer response (e.g., "tenant unions") and the extent to which these organizations constitute, in effect, a form of rent control.

Section 508.06. Neighborhood and Marketing Area

In discussing the neighborhood in which the property is located, the appraiser should narratively explain the factors that define the market area of the property. The appraiser should consider "comparison shopping alternatives" for the typical tenant, including both rental and ownership opportunities. In addition, the appraiser should include the following information:

- A map highlighting the property site, major competing rental developments, the highway network serving the neighborhood, major employment centers, etc., and outlining the market area of the property. The map should be attached to the appraiser's report.
- Describe major rental competition of the property within the market area in addition to the three comparables required. In analyzing competition, the appraiser should consider and report on: project name; location; year opened; number of units; bedroom mix; unit size; lease term; rental rate per square foot (per month and per annum); vacancy; furnished or unfurnished; rental history; open space and recreational facilities; utilities; type construction; number of stories; and condition of improvements.
- Inventory

  Immediate Inventory—Report on completed rental units in the market area not leased. Indicate how many units will be on the market during the property's rent-up period.

Developing Inventory—Report on rental properties in the area already under construction or on which construction is expected to begin during the property's rent-up period, and evaluate the competitive impact on the property.

Potential Inventory—Identify and evaluate timing and competitive significance of potential inventory, based on interviews with knowledgeable representatives of the housing industry.

The appraiser's conclusions regarding supply and demand should be in the form of a summary of the anticipated competitive position and marketability of the property's rental units and a projection of the anticipated rent-up period for recently completed or moderate rehabilitation property based on the facts developed in analyzing Market Area and Neighborhood.

Section 508.07. Site

The appraiser should consider and comment on the following factors relevant to an assessment of the property site:

- Whether the size, shape and topography of the site is adequate to accommodate the existing or planned improvements to the property, including on-site parking and recreational facilities.
- Whether buildings at the site are located to provide privacy and maximum open area. Density of development should be carefully analyzed; overcrowding could adversely affect the competitive position of the property now and in the future.
- Whether the site has adequate street frontage for ease and safety of ingress and egress, and for view and appearance. The appraiser should consider the type of street leading to the property site, including its width, speed limit, traffic flow during peak periods, service or deceleration lanes, traffic lights or stop signs.
- Whether parking of a minimum of one space per apartment is provided at the site. Fannie Mae prefers one space per bedroom. If the site does not meet these standards, the appraiser should document any reasons for an exception. Parking spaces should be easily accessible to apartment entrances. Parking surfaces should be paved.
- Whether the property site is located in a FEMA (formerly HUD) designated Flood Hazard area. If so, the appraiser should comment on the effect of such location.
- In connection with the section in Form 1050 for "Site Improvements" (water, sewer, electricity, gas, etc.), the appraiser should be aware that "public utility services" means services supplied by a governmentally-owned, supported, or regulated entity. Community or neighborhood systems sponsored, owned, or

operated by a developer or a private company and that are not regulated or financed by the government are not included in the term "public utility services."

If the site is served by such a privately-owned water system, the appraiser should check the box for "private well," cross out the word "well," and substitute the word "water." For a private sewer system, check the box for "septic tank," cross out the words "septic tank," and insert "private sewer." The appraiser should notify the Lender immediately of this circumstance as public water and sewer are required under Delegated Underwriting and Servicing.

Whether there exist, to the appraiser's knowledge, environmental hazards or any hazardous conditions on the property or within the immediate vicinity of the property that affect the value of the property. Such hazards include the presence of hazardous wastes, toxic substances, asbestos-containing materials, urea-formaldehyde insulation, radon air pollution, and similar environmental hazards. The appraiser should call any such items found during the appraisal process to the attention of the Lender and comment on the effect of any hazardous conditions on the property's value and marketability and make appropriate adjustments in his or her overall valuation of the property.

Section 508.08. Description of Improvement

The appraiser must provide a complete and detailed description of existing or planned improvements to the property in the applicable spaces on Form 1050 or in an addendum attached to the report.

The appraiser should make a general evaluation of the quality of construction of the property. The quality of construction should match or exceed prevailing standards in the community in which the property is located. The appraiser must comment on any violations of building, health, fire or safety codes at the property.

The appraiser should give special attention to the adequacy of insulation in the property's walls, ceilings, and roof to provide energy conservation. If the quality or quantity of insulation is inadequate, the appraiser should discuss the cost of improvement in relation to the potential for increased rentals and decreased operating costs at the property.

If the appraiser judges that the property is structurally deficient or the quality of the electrical service, plumbing and mechanical equipment is questionable, the appraiser must so advise the Lender.

The appraiser must also suggest improvements to the unit mix, size and layout in light of his or her market analysis. The appraiser should specifically comment on the adequacy of closets, tenants' storage, laundry facilities, tenants' services, recreational facilities, etc. The appraiser is reminded that his or her analysis of the property's structure and components must be reflected in both the charge for depreciation and in calculating operating costs.

Section 508.09. Cost Approach to Valuation

The appraiser must use all three approaches to market value—sales comparison, replacement cost, and income capitilization—in preparing the valuation.

The appraiser must prepare a Land Value Estimate. In valuing the land according to the cost approach, Fannie Mae recommends the appraiser use the Market Data Approach (comparison to, and analysis of, sales of similar sites). The appraiser must describe all factors affecting the Land Value Estimate. Comparable land sales must be identified on the Market Area Map.

The appraiser should also prepare a Replacement Cost Estimate. The source of replacement cost factors should be identified, e.g., actual contracts, cost manuals, cost in place studies, etc. Items in the Replacement Cost Estimate should be calculated by square foot and these calculations should be shown. Unenclosed or unroofed area (e.g., balconies) are to be excluded from the building area calculations, but are to be calculated and reported separately with applicable cost factors. Paved areas for parking, driveways and walks are also to be calculated and reported separately with appropriate unit costs. The appraiser should attach an analysis breaking down the various forms of depreciation, including dollar amount and justification. The final value estimate is to be based on completion of all needed repairs, which the appraiser must list.

If there is a ground lease, the Lender's underwriter must provide the appraiser with a copy of the Multifamily Ground Lease Analysis (Form No. 461), which the appraiser must complete. All value calculations are to be shown.

Section 508.10. Comparable Rental Data

The appraiser must analyze all competitive market rentals and provide data on no less than three comparables. Comparability will take into consideration attributes of projects which demonstrate similar locational characteristics such as schools, shopping, and transportation; tenant user categories such as single people, married couples, and the elderly: projects which are physically similar in building structure type, considering garden, low-rise, and elevator structures; available amenities for tenant use such as recreation facilities; and unit types, sizes and mix most similar to the subject property.

Section 508.11. Monthly Rent Schedule

In calculating the scheduled or economic rental income of a property, Fannie Mae's standard is that the appraiser will recognize all project income generated from both residential and commercial (limited to 20% of effective gross income) tenant usage with the exceptions that income attributable to furniture rental, pet fees, forfeited security deposits and similar income is not allowable.

The Lender will provide the appraiser with a Certification to Project Rent Roll

(Fannie Mae Form 4243) not more than 30 days old at the time of loan application (see Section 304, item 14). The rent roll must show occupant's name, unit type, apartment number, monthly rental, lease expiration date, and whether the apartment is furnished or unfurnished. The Lender will also supply and the appraiser will analyze current income and expense statements of the property for the previous three years, if available. For recently completed properties (which have not achieved sustaining occupancy) where such history is not available, a market study must be done and the underwriting analysis based on a pro forma statement.

For the Scheduled Rent Sections, the appraiser must calculate an existing property's rental income based upon its current certified rent roll. For recently completed or moderately rehabilitated buildings, the appraiser may use a current rent roll and pro forma to justify the rents along with information on current rate of lease-up and market rental comparables.

For the Economic Rent Section, the appraiser should recognize economic rents and attendant expenses that would be achievable at the time of the appraisal and should not trend rents to any future date. The appraiser may use the highest rents at which units are being turned over as part of a rent increase program, or the rents the subject units could command in the open market.

Loans secured by properties located in rent control areas are eligible for purchase. Rent control legislation may, however, jeopardize the quality of a multifamily mortgage investment. The appraiser must research existing or proposed rent control legislation affecting a property and evaluate the impact of the legislation on the investment.

If a portion of the property's income stream comes from subsidies, the Appraiser should carefully evaluate the quantity and the quality of the subsidy payment. In this case, the appraiser must include a narrative analysis on the affect the subsidy will have on the value of the property during the term of the mortgage. If the subsidy payments raise the rent level of the property above the market rate, the quantity, quality, and duration of the subsidy is an even more critical underwriting concern.

The appraiser must also determine that rents attained at the property are not the result of monetary or other concessions. If concessions are granted, the appraiser must determine the reason for the concession and whether this practice is limited to the subject property or widespread in the market. This also means that the appraiser must discount the subject rents on an annualized basis before they are capitalized into a value determination. If rental concessions are prevalent in a market area, this fact must be carefully considered in relationship to the rent comparables used and the vacancy factor indicated in the market.

Section 508.12 Market Approach to Value

The market approach to value calls for comparison of the subject property to three similar projects, located within a reasonable distance, that have been sold within recent months prior to the date of the appraisal. In obtaining data on comparables, the appraiser should be certain that the transactions used were made at arm's length between buyer and seller. A sale between relatives or between individuals working for the same company or for companies held by the same company is obviously not desirable for use as a comparable. The appraiser may also have to adjust for financing through the use of cash equivalency. The reviewer should be satisfied that each comparable used is similar to the subject with regard to age, size, condition, amenities, and tenant user profile. Further, the comparable properties should be located in the same neighborhood as the subject or in areas that are physically similar and catering to the same market. The derivation of the gross rent multiplier must reflect any adjustments made to comparable sales prices for cash equivalency.

Section 508.13. Vacancy and Credit Loss

Fannie Mae requires the appraiser to consider a vacancy and credit loss allowance in the calculation of income from residential units. If the actual vacancy rate and credit loss for the property is 5% or less, a minimum allowance of 5% must be used. If the actual vacancy rate and credit loss is higher, the appraiser must use the higher rate unless convinced that actions within the market and the management ability of the borrower will bring the property to a vacancy and credit loss of 5% or less within the next 6 month period.

Section 508.14. Expenses

In determining a property's operating expenses, the appraiser must estimate expenses over the next 12 months. They should use operating history of the property over the past three years if available. Emphasis should be placed upon the most recent 12-month period preceding the date of the appraisal. Where there is a major difference between the actual and forecasted expenses, the appraiser must explain this difference with regard to each expense item.

All expense items listed in Form 1050 are important and require the appraiser's careful consideration. However, Fannie Mae believes it is particularly important for the appraiser to provide specific comments on the following expense items:

- Real Estate Taxes—If the property has been recently completed, the appraiser's estimate of the eventual tax assessment must be fully supported by attaching an analysis of comparable properties. Where available, a letter from the local Tax Assessor's office as to the proposed assessment would be desirable. The tax estimate for appraisal purposes must reflect current tax rates and assessments, as well as historical information, unless the appraiser knows of an imminent change in either the rate or the assessment of taxes.

- Other taxes and assessments—This category would include those taxes and assessments that can become liens against the real estate, excluding assessments for capital improvements. For each item listed, comment by the appraiser is required.
- Insurance—The appraiser should consider the insurance requirements described in Chapter 8 of this Part. Local requirements will dictate some additional types of insurance coverages and amounts of coverage as appropriate and necessary for the property. The appraiser must calculate the cost of insurance required by this Guide on an annual basis and substantiate the calculation by verification with insuring companies.
- Fuel, Gas, and Electricity—The appraiser must report and substantiate these items individually. Estimates can be substantiated by an analysis of historical data, by discussions with appropriate officials of utility companies, or by examination of operating statements of comparable properties. The portion of the gas or electricity that is used for heating or air conditioning is to be included under "Fuel."

  The appraiser should also comment as to whether gas and electricity are metered separately to each individual unit or are on a common meter. The appraiser should also comment on the feasibility and cost of conversion to separate meters and indicate the general industry practice regarding metering in the market area.
- Water and Sewer—The calculation of these charges must be substantiated as previously discussed above under "Fuel, Gas, and Electricity."
- Building Maintenance and Repairs—The appraiser must itemize expenses and costs and support this itemization by identifying sources of information. In examining operating statements, the appraiser must annualize expenses and eliminate capital expenditures that would normally be included in replacement reserves.
- Non-resident Management—Fees paid for off-site management and leasing should be typical for the market area and calculated on an annualized basis.
- Salaried employees—The function and number of employees at the property must relate to the needs of prudent management and be supported by analysis of comparable properties. If the rental value of a resident manager's or other employee's apartment is included in the gross rental projection, the appraisal must deduct such rental value as an expense charge.
- Advertising, telephone, legal and audit—These expenses are often listed as administration expenses on operating statements and the appraiser should try to differentiate the appropriate expense item. These line items should not include any partnership expenses, e.g., a partnership audit. Advertising expense should be for the property only and not for other properties managed by the same management entity.

The appraiser should estimate an initial deposit and an annual deposit to the replacement reserve based upon the remaining economic life of individual components. Carpeting, drapes, ranges, refrigerators, dishwashers and disposals are treated as short term items and are to be depreciated over their remaining economic life. Heating and air conditioning units will be treated in accordance with normal longevity of the HVAC system being used at the property. The appraiser should also consider paving and roofing. The remaining economic life method of estimating the replacement reserve need not be used on recently completed properties unless the appraiser or Lender considers it necessary.

The minimum annual reserve for replacement amount is $150.00 per unit.

After the appraiser has completed the estimate of the initial deposit and annual deposits to the reserve for replacement based upon the remaining economic life method, the appraiser will compare the estimated annual deposits to the $150.00 per unit amount. If the appraiser determines that a higher figure should be indicated. A higher figure is more likely where the property is older and has not been moderately or substantially rehabilitated.

Section 508.15. Income Approach to Value and Commercial Income Analysis

The income approach to value, which entails the capitalization of the property's income stream, is often the predominant indicator of value. The appraiser must use two methods of determining the capitalization rate. The first method is extraction of the rate from current market transactions of comparable properties. The second method is the derivation of a blended rate based upon the proposed project financing (based on yield, not on a discounted rate) and an equity dividend rate supported by market data. In the second instance, the appraiser should make no additional adjustment either for project appreciation or depreciation. The appraiser must correlate the two indicators to arrive at the most supportable rate to be used in capitalizing the project income stream into the value derived through the income approach.

If a property contains commercial space, the appraiser is to segregate the income and expenses attributable to that space and capitalize the non-residential net operating income separately from that of the residential income attributable to the property. Effective gross non-residential income used in this calculation may not exceed 20% of total effective gross income. The following are Fannie Mae's guidelines regarding analysis of commercial lease(s):

1. All leases must have an original term of three years or more. Any leases with remaining terms of less than one year must show proof of lease renewal or the affected space must be included in the vacancy calculation. If a tenant is an established ongoing business in an option period, it will be left to the

discretion of the appraiser to determine the likelihood of continued lease income from that space.

2. All lease payments must be supported by market comparables. If the payment is at a contract rent that is less than market then the contract rent must be used. No consideration will be given to income that is based upon a percentage of gross sales or any type of participation clause in the lease; only base rent will be considered.
3. The vacancy factor must consider the typical rate in the market, the existing conditions of the immediate neighborhood and the condition and history of the property. In no case will the vacancy factor used in the analysis be less than 10%.
4. The expenses must be supported with appropriate market data, must include those expenses typical for the tenant user, and will reflect any special conditions indicated in the lease that would reduce the net income of the property.
5. The quality of the tenant and the duration of the income stream must be carefully analyzed and consideration must be given to the location of the commercial space as it relates to a commercial user versus a residential user. Among the locational considerations are parking, access, and street exposure. In addition, the flexibility and configuration of the leasable space is critical to allow for changes over a period of time for multiple tenant users.

The appraiser should provide a calculation for the percentage of net rentable commercial rental area compared to total net rentable area of the project. This calculation is for underwriting purposes. The percentage of commercial net rentable area is determined by dividing commercial net rentable area by the total net rentable area of the project.

Based upon the quality and duration of the commercial income, the appraiser may use a discounted cash flow method for valuing *only* the commercial spaces in the valuation process. If this method is used, the appraiser must fully document the discount rate and the capitalization rate with current market data.

The leased fee value contribution of the commercial space must be shown as a separate value and as part of the total value of the property.

Section 508.16 Conclusions

In the space on Form 1050 for "Reconciliation and Value Conclusion," the appraiser should enter the dollar amount estimated using each of the three approaches to value. In the space titled "Final Reconciliation," the appraiser should state a conclusion as to the final market value of the property and include a short narrative summary of the rationale for arriving at this final valuation.

The appraiser must indicate in the space for "Conditions & Requirements of Appraisal", the "as is" value of the property, if appropriate, or a recommendation for any required repairs, replacements, etc. The appraiser may attach information or exhibits to fully explain any conditions or requirements of the appraisal.

The appraisal report must be dated and signed by the appraiser who inspected the property. The signature date should be the date the appraiser completed the assignment. The date of the valuation must be a current date and not projected into the future.

INDEX